Library of
Davidson College

Linguistische Arbeiten 16

Herausgegeben von Herbert E. Brekle, Hans Jürgen Heringer,
Christian Rohrer, Heinz Vater und Otmar Werner

Sr. Mary-John Mananzan, OSB

The »Language Game« of Confessing One's Belief

A Wittgensteinian-Austinian Approach
to the Linguistic Analysis of Creedal Statements

Max Niemeyer Verlag
Tübingen 1974

*To my mother and my sister
in deep gratitude for their abiding love*

ISBN 3-484-10199-7

© Max Niemeyer Verlag Tübingen 1974
Alle Rechte vorbehalten. Ohne ausdrückliche Genehmigung des Verlages ist es auch nicht gestattet, dieses Buch oder Teile daraus auf photomechanischem Wege zu vervielfältigen. Printed in Germany

ACKNOWLEDGEMENTS

I wish to thank the many generous people who have given me their support and help in writing this thesis. I am grateful, first of all, to my Superiors for having given me the opportunity to go on higher studies. To Fr. Carlo Huber, S. J. my very special thanks for his guidance, criticism and unfailing encouragement. To Prof. Dorothy Emmet and Dr. Nicholas Lash, who helped me in the difficult task of choosing a suitable topic, I happily acknowledge my indebtedness. I also thank Sr. Caridad Barrion, OSB, my former teacher, and my friend, Sr. M. Evelyn Jegen, for their patient proofreading of the manuscript and for their helpful suggestions. My thanks are due also to my co-sisters, Sr. M. Irmlinde Geiselmann and Sr. M. Columbana Käfer for sharing the burden of preparing the final mimeographed script. Finally, I wish to thank everyone, who, in one way or another, has given me help - inspirational, critical, and technical.

As St. Benedict would say, this work was made possible "with the help of many brethren."

TABLE OF CONTENTS

LIST OF ABBREVIATIONS   XI
INTRODUCTION   1

PART ONE: THE LINGUISTIC TURN

Chapter I.
A CRITICAL SURVEY OF THE LINGUISTIC ANALYSES OF RELIGIOUS LANGUAGE   7
Wittgenstein and Religious Language   8
    The *Tractatus*
    The *Philosophical Investigations*
The Logical-Positivistic Treatment of Religious Language   10
    Alfred Jules Ayer
    Antony Flew
    Appraisal
Non-Cognitive Treatment of Creedal Statements   15
    John Wisdom
    Richard Hare
    R.F. Holland
    R.B. Braithwaite
    Appraisal
The Cognitive Treatment of Creedal Statements   22
    I.M. Crombie
    John Hick
    John Macquarrie
    E.L. Mascall
    Appraisal
Functional-Situational Approach to Creedal Statements   31
    Dallas High
    William Hordern

VIII

    Ferré, Poteat, Coburn
    Appraisal

Chapter II.
METHODOLOGICAL CONSIDERATIONS   40
The Wittgensteinian Approach to Linguistic Analysis   40
    Linguistic Analysis in the *Tractatus*
    Wittgenstein's Later Views on Linguistic Analysis
Wittgensteinian Approach to Religious Belief   48
    In the *Tractatus*
    In the *Lectures and Conversations* and *Philosophical Investigations*
J.L. Austin and the Analysis of Statements   50
    The Performative Theory
    The Force Theory
The Adoption of Wittgensteinian and Austinian Methodology in this Thesis   56

PART TWO: THE LINGUISTIC ANALYSIS OF CREEDAL STATEMENTS

Chapter III.
THE INNER DYNAMIC OF CREEDAL STATEMENTS   59
Creedal Statements in the Context of the Christian Life   59
    The Official Uses of the Creed
    Private Uses of the Creed
The Creeds in Christian Tradition   63
    The Uses of the Creeds in the Early Church
    The Rise of Synodal Creeds
    The Creeds in Later Church History
Digression A: Non-Christian Uses of Confessional Creeds   70
The Varying Forces of Creedal Statements   73
    Locutionary Forces of Creedal Statements
    Illocutionary Forces of Creedal Statements
    Perlocutionary Forces of Creedal Statements
Digression B: Dogmatic Statements as Creedal Statements   76

Chapter IV.
THE LINGUISTIC TOPOGRAPHY OF CREEDAL STATEMENTS   78

Creedal Statements Linked with Everyday Language	78
Expression of Belief	
Expression of Knowledge	
Promise-Vow-Pledge Statements	
Creedal Statements Compared with Non-Religious Uses of Language	85
Scientific Discourse	
Philosophical Discourse	
Ethical Discourse	
Aesthetic Discourse	
Poetical Discourse	
Political Discourse	
Creedal Statements within Religious Discourse	101
Prayer Utterances	
The Language of Morals	
Narrative and Reporting Statements	
Preaching and Catechizing	
Theological Discourse	
Sacramental Formulae	
Mystical Language	
Conclusion	
Chapter V.	
THE QUESTION OF "MEANING" AND "TRUTH" REGARDING CREEDAL STATEMENTS	111
The Different Uses of "Meaning"	112
The Informative Potentiality of Creedal Statements	114
The Reference Aspect of Creedal Statements	115
Reference Proposals for the Concept "God"	
Modes of Reference of Religious Proposals	
The Truth Aspect of Creedal Statements	121
The Varied Uses of "Truth"	
The Notion of "Grammatical Claims"	
The Grammatical Function of Creedal Statements	
Chapter VI.	
THE "FORM OF LIFE" OF CREEDAL STATEMENTS	129
The Primary Presuppositions of the Christian Way of Life	130
The Theistic Presupposition	

    The Christological Presupposition
Factors that Condition Creedal Statements   132
    The Faith-Character of the Christian Way of Life
    The Social Aspect of the Christian Way of Life
    The Missionary Factor
    The Liturgical Aspect
The Internal Justification of Creedal Statements   139
The Significance of the Christian Religious Discourse   143

CONCLUSION   150
BIBLIOGRAPHY   156
APPENDIX   171

LIST OF ABBREVIATIONS

Note: The use of numbers with the following abbreviations indicates paragraph numbers in the case of the works of Wittgenstein (BB, PI, TLP, OC) and the documents (AG, DS) unless preceded by "p" or "pp". In the case of RGG, the number indicates the columns. For the remaining works (SM, HDTW), the number indicates the pages.

AG — "Ad Gentes" in W. Abbot (ed.) *The Documents of Vatican II*. New York: Guild Press, 1966, 584-630.

BB — Ludwig Wittgenstein, *The Blue and Brown Books*. Oxford: Basil Blackwell, 1958.

DS — Denzinger-Schönmetzer. Symbolorum definitionum et declarationum de rebus fidei et morum. Barcinone: Herder, 1967.

HDTW — J.L. Austin. *How To Do Things With Words*. ed. J.O. Urmson. London: Oxford University Press, 1967.

OC — Ludwig Wittgenstein, *On Certainty*. ed. by G.E.M. Anscombe and G.H. von Wright. Oxford: Basil Blackwell, 1969.

PI — Ludwig Wittgenstein, *Philosophical Investigations*. German with English translation by G.E.M. Anscombe. Oxford: Basil Blackwell, 1953.

RGG — *Religion in der Geschichte und Gegenwart*. Tübingen: J.C.B. Mohr, 1957.

SM — Karl Rahner (ed.) *Sacramentum Mundi*. Freiburg: Herder, 1969.

TLP — Ludwig Wittgenstein, *Tractatus Logico-Philosophicus*. German with English translation by C.K. Ogdon and F.P. Ramsey with an introduction by B. Russell. London: Routledge and Kegan Paul, 1922.

INTRODUCTION

The fascination with language is as old as the fascination of man with
himself. Very early in the history of philosophy, Aristotle had already
characterized man as "*zoon logon echon.*"[1] Speech is indeed a distinguishing
feature of man. But just as it is with many familiar things, it becomes
obscure by its familiarity. One uses language almost without reflection
that one is using it. But since it is a "human existential mode of being
a man in the world and thus of knowing reality and ordering it,"[2] a lack
of reflection on how it functions can lead to conceptual problems and
even to errors of judgement which have, of course, practical consequences.
In Wittgensteinian terms, one can find oneself like a fly imprisoned in
a bottle. (PI, 284,and 309) This predicament is perhaps most felt in
philosophy, although the other human sciences do not altogether escape it.
But since philosophy primarily deals with concepts, it is most prone, if
no attention is paid to the workings of language, to be caught in a web
of conceptual tangles which can appear as philosophical problems.

 The history of philosophy shows how philosophical discourses could go
about endlessly in circles all the time sounding profound and brilliant.
It is the merit of the modern linguistic philosophers beginning with G.E.
Moore to play the role of the little child in the old fairy tale about
the king's invisible robe, to shout amidst naive admirers of esoteric
philosophizing: "But that is profound nonsense!" Further on, Ludwig Wittgenstein and also J.L. Austin, each in his own way, would show how many such
"philosophical problems" just disappear as soon as the workings of language
are clarified. Modern linguistic philosophy is thus "linguistic" in the
sense of being constantly aware of the presence of language, which means,
negatively, being sensitive to the danger of being misled by words and

---

1 Cf. Pol. A 2. 1253 a 9/10, H 13. 1332 b 4/5

2 C. Huber,*Schematic Notes for Fundamental Critics* . (Rome: Gregoriana,
 1971), 86.

trapped into hollow verbal arguments, and positively, by being aware "that
in discussing, as philosophy always has, the relations between concepts
and the nature of various ideas, one always comes back to the expression
of such things in the human activity of thinking and talking about the
world."[3]

This insight of linguistic philosophy cannot but have repercussions
on the sciences that concern themselves with any form of locution. Christian
theology with its preoccupation with the "Word", its interpretation and
communication, is therefore likewise influenced by these philosophical
insights. The philosophy of religion which provides a prolegomena for
theology[4], is directly affected by it, because on it falls the task of
clarifying the concepts used in religion. The new insight about the importance of observing the functioning of language in the clarification of
concepts has given its approach a linguistic turn. It focuses its attention therefore on the religious use of language.[5]

This study is an attempt to make use of the new philosophical insights
in the effort to understand the phenomenon of belief, specifically on the
Christian belief. This phenomenon is being tirelessly studied by different
methods and by different disciplines. This work aims to contribute to this
never-ending effort, by taking the newly opened path of linguistic analysis.
It will take as object of the study one aspect of the phenomenon, namely,
the linguistic act of "confessing one's belief" and it will proceed by
focusing its attention on the linguistic "crystallization" of this act -
the creedal statements. The phrase "creedal statement" in its strict sense
means a statement taken from the Church's official creedal formulae.

---

3 B. Williams and A. Montefiore, *British Analytical Philosophy* (London:
Routledge and Kegan Paul, 1966), 7-8.

4 This is the main argument of Karl Rahner's book: *Hörer des Wortes: Zur
Grundlegung einer Religionsphilosophie* (München: Kösel Verlag, 1963).

5 The phrase "religious use of language" is used by Dallas High rather
than just "religious language" in order to emphazise the fact that
there is no language exclusive to religion, but that the same "human
language may be used to carry out various linguistic tasks or execute
various religious performances: pray, worship, name a god or gods or
God, prescribe action, relate a myth or a story... recount history,
sing the Nunc Dimittis or say creeds." Cf. Dallas High, *Language, Persons and Belief* (New York: Oxford University Press, 1967), 135. In this
work, however, once the above explanation has become clear, the phrase
"religious language" and "religious use of language" will be used inter-
changeable to mean the same thing.

In its broader meaning, however, it includes the believer's expressions of his faith or what philosophers take to be so. Here an attempt will be made to study its varying nuances.

In order to understand the concern, approach and method of this study, it is necessary to set the stage by clarifying some key terms. In his introductory contribution to the eighty-fourth annual meeting of the American Catholic Philosophical Association, Ernon McMullin provides a valuable clarification of terms. First he points out the difference between "analytical method" and "analytical philosophy".
Every school of philosophy uses at one time or the other some analytic method. But the title "analytic" is reserved for a philosophy "whose central insight it si that the human mind can attain to no general explanatory scheme of the kind Metaphysics has always purported to be."[6]

With regard to "analytic method", one should distinguish the kind of analysis used. A philosophical question, for example, can be subjected to *logical analysis* to clarify its logical form, discover its conceptual confusions or reveal its semantic assumptions concerning reality. Experience can be analysed *phenomenologically* by revealing its central structures and describing it in general terms. One can likewise show the *psychological* motivations and subconscious drives behind a philosophical question or statement. There is thus not one unique analytic method. The family of analytic methods may be distinguished by contrasting them with a system-building, axiomatic-deductive or purely intuitive approach.[7]

In the contemporary philosophical scene, the phrase "philosophical analysis" is reserved to analysis which has some sort of linguistic or semantic basis. The two that concern us here are the so-called *reductive analysis* and *linguistic analysis*, particularly the latter. Reductive analysis has been the principal instrument of the logical atomism of the early Russell, of the logical positivism of the Vienna Circle, and the artificial language construction of the later Carnap. None of these is analytic philosophy properly so called. They are reductively analytic in their approach to language in that they hold that ordinary language

---

6 E. McMullin, "The Analytical Approach to Philosophy" in *Proceedings of the American Catholic Philosophical Association*, vol. 34. (Washington D.C.: Catholic University of America Press, 1966), 51.

7 *Ibid.*, 52 ff.

is an inefficient tool of expression and communication and is ill suited to the purposes of philosophy, because it gives rise to misunderstandings. They propose therefore that the diversities of natural language be reduced to a small set of artificial logical forms which would display the basic types of logical connectives and syntactical categories.[8] It must be said at once that this is not the kind of analysis that will be used in this work.

The other type of philosophical analysis which is the method chosen by this study is the so-called "linguistic analysis". Unlike the former, this form of analysis concentrated its reflection on ordinary language rather than using its efforts in constructing language models. In this context, "analysis" ranges from a simple inspection of the claim made to a more complex distinction between and comparison of different meanings of the expressions involved in order to find out the patterns of interrelations that the understandings of the statements involve. A more detailed treatment of the method, the reason for its use, how far and in what way it will be used, will be the burden of a separat chapter on Methodology. Here it is only to be emphasized that philosophical linguistic analysis will be used in this study *as a method*, prescinding from its other philosophical presuppositions or claims which do not affect its workings as a method.

An explanation of the different chapters and the way they are ordered is still called for. The work is divided into two main parts. The first part entitled "The Linguistic Turn" aims to provide the historical and methodological background for the study. In the first chapter, a survey of the work already done along the line of linguistic analysis of religious discourse will show the positive results of these studies, but will likewise point out where some have gone into blind alleys. These positive and negative aspects have been taken into consideration in this work's own investigations. The next chapter then selects and explains the insights and methods deemed most suitable for the specific task of this thesis. The philosophy of language of both Wittgenstein and Austin are discussed in so far as they provide or affect the methods adopted by this study.

---

[8] *Ibid*, 53.

The second part of the work is the actual study of the chosen subject matter. This principal part consists of four chapters. The first of these surveys the uses of creedal statements both in the present Christian (Roman Catholic) way of life and in the Christian tradition. According to these uses, the creedal utterances are distinguished as forms of speech acts emitting, each, another linguistic force. In the next chapter, a comparison of the creedal statement with other forms of statements occurring in human discourse in general and likewise with other forms of utterances in the context of religious discourse itself, is made. This is done to map out the contours, so to say, of creedal statements showing how they overlap with other uses of language, but at the same time isolating their characteristic aspects which make them a distinct form of utterance.

The characterization of the internal and external aspects of creedal statements, necessarily leads to the question of "meaning", because creedal statements are a use of language and the concept of language primarily includes the aspect of meaning. Here it is necessary to note that the creedal statements will not be hermeneutically treated. The meaning of the content of the individual articles of the creed will not be analysed as such. This task belongs to theology. The concern here will be the question of *meaningfulness* of creedal statements. The content of the individual concepts occuring in the statement will be treated only in so far as it illuminates this specific concern. Finally, the main features of the form of life in which the confession of one's belief takes place will be discussed to round up the efforts to understand this specific form of speech act.

From these reflections, conclusions regarding creedal statements as speech acts are drawn and consequences pointed out both for philosophy of religion and for theology.

PART ONE

THE LINGUISTIC TURN

Chapter I

A CRITICAL SURVEY OF THE LINGUISTIC ANALYSES OF RELIGIOUS LANGUAGE

Explanation of the language used in talking about God has occupied the minds of theologians at least as far back as Augustine. The contemporary philosophical preoccupation about religious language, which has its roots in modern British empiricism and modern logic, is, however, new in its impulse, in its approach and in its intentions. Out of G.E. Moore's and B. Russell's reaction to the Hegel-inspired pompous metaphysics of Bradley, Bosanquet and McTaggart arose the philosophical method of linguistic analysis which has subsequently assumed many forms and has dominated the philosophical scene in the past fifty to sixty years in the Anglo-Saxon countries. As a method, it has penetrated into other disciplines - into the political and social sciences, into the humanities and most especially, it has exerted quite an influence on the philosophy of religion and theology.

It is the purpose of this chapter to make an evaluative survey of the different ways in which linguistic analysis has been used in the treatment of religious language. This will provide the background for this work's own attempt to focus on one specific religious use of language - that of confessing one's belief.

The survey will be systematic rather than chronological, although chronology has not been entirely disregarded. In the classification of the different approaches, those which appeared first in the philosophical scene are treated first but authors of more or less the same position are grouped together regardless of the chronology in the appearance of their work. It is important to note that there are no definite lines separating the groups of analysts. In fact, various authors classify the analysts in different ways. The classification made here shows a progression in the development of the understanding of religious language. From the logical positivistic rejection of religious talk, as meaningless statements, sprang the effort of analysts to save it by emphasizing its non-cognitive aspects which escape the positivistic ban. This in turn would provoke the reaction of subsequent analysts to re-emphasize the cognitive aspect. Sensing the inadequacy of previous approaches, a more contemporary group would adopt a new approach based on other presuppositions and inspired by the insights of Ludwig Wittgenstein.

Holding the key to modern philosophical activity of linguistic analysis is undoubtedly the inspired and passionate genius of Ludwig Wittgenstein. It is therefore necessary first to discuss his philosophical insights in order to understand the analysts of religious language.

I. *Wittgenstein and Religious Language*

The philosophy of Wittgenstein has two phases, the earlier phase, which is expressed by the *Tractatus Logico-Philosophicus*[1] and the later phase which culminated in the *Philosophical Investigations*[2]. Most of the linguistic analyses done in this century are either a prolongation or a reaction to his early thoughts or application of or developments inspired by his later views.[3]

1. The Tractatus Logico-Philosophicus

The *Tractatus*, published in 1921 in Germany, has seven main propositions. The first two offer the ontological foundation of the theories that follow them. The world is to be seen constituted by a totality of facts and not of things. (TLP, 1.1) In the third thesis, there is a going over from ontology to epistemology in which a relation is made between the world and the thoughts about the world. In the fourth thesis begins the investigation of language treating significant propositions as means of formulating thoughts. In the fifth and sixth proposition, the internal structure of

---

1 Ludwig Wittgenstein, *Tractatus Logico-Philosophicus*, German with English translation by C.K. Ogden and F.P. Ramsey with an introduction by B. Russell (London: Routledge and Kegan Paul, 1922).

2 Ludwig Wittgenstein, *Philosophical Investigations*, German with English translation by G.E.M. Anscombe (Oxford: Basil Blackwell, 1953).

3 This is especially true of the logical-positivistic analysts who were influenced by Wittgenstein's early thoughts on language and of the more contemporary analysts grouped in the "Functional-Situational Approach to Creedal Statements" in this thesis. Cf. "Logical Positivism" in *Encyclopedia of Philosophy*, 1st ed., V, 52; and Dallas High, *New Essays in Religious Language* (New York: Oxford University Press, 1961), Introduction.

language is analysed and a general pattern is constructed to which every
significant proposition must conform. The book ends with a grim and uncompromisingly consequent pronouncement which condemns to eternal silence
all manner of talk not fitting this pattern, itself along with these. The
following gives a rough sketch of the main theories of the *Tractatus* and
how these are related to one another:

> The boldest summary of Wittgenstein's conception might run as follows:
> Reality (the world) is a *mosaic* of independent items - the *atomic
> facts*: each of these is like a *chain*, in which objects (logical
> simples) 'hang in one another'; the objects are connected in a
> *network* of logical possibilities ('logical space'); the simplest
> 'elementary propositions' are pictures of atomic facts, themselves
> facts in which names are concatenated, and all other propositions
> are truth functions of the elementary ones; language is the great
> *mirror* in which the logical network is reflected, 'shown' mani-
> fested.[4]

Within this system, there are only three forms of meaningful propositions,
namely: (1) tautologies (2) contradictions and (3) descriptive propositions. The first two do not say anything (TLP, 4.461). The descriptive
proposition can only say that a certain state of affairs exists or not.
Meaningful talk limits itself therefore to statements about states of
affairs.

Now one begins to see where theological talk comes in, or rather does
not come in. Theological propositions lie beyond the boundaries set up
for thoughts and language - they lie beyond the world. They are not expressions of some state of affairs in the world. Furthermore they cannot
be univocally stated, because a univocal is to be found only in the realms
of empirical facts. They cannot be put into words, (TLP, 6.522) and should
therefore be passed over in silence. (TLP, 7).

2. The Philosophical Investigations

Reaction to the *Tractatus* was animatedly varied. It ushered in what
may be called the polemical period of linguistic analysis. The main controversy centered on the meaninglessness/meaningfulness of religious
language. Meanwhile, Wittgenstein had come to new insights about language
which are set down in his posthumously published work, *The Philosophical
Investigations*. Just as in the case of the *Tractatus* , so also would this

---

4 Max Black, *A Companion to Wittgenstein's Tractatus* (Cambridge: University Press, 1954), 3.

book usher in a new era in linguistic analysis. In it, Wittgenstein refutes the main propositions of his earlier work: the onlological foundation of his theory of language, the picture theory of meaning and logical anlysis. Among the positive aspects of the book are the insight about the meaning of a word consisting in its "use in the language" (PI,43), the idea of "language games" (PI,7) which regards language as an activity in a "form of life" (PI,23) based on tacit presuppositions within the context of which statements take on validity. These ideas will be treated in detail in the chapter on method, since they constitute the main method used in this work. Here it suffices to mention that the *Philosophical Investigations* lifted the ban on religious talk imposed by the *Tractatus*.

This programmatic work, together with the ideas on the religious belief which Wittgenstein expressed in lectures, the note of which are published posthumously in a small volume, *Lectures and Conversations on Aesthetics, Psychology and Religious Belief*[5], form the basis, the inspiration and the starting point of the more recent forms of linguistic analysis of religious language.

II. *The Logical-Positivistic Treatment of Religious Language*

The first type of linguistic analysis to be treated here is the logical-positivistic form, which was influenced by the thoughts of the early Wittgenstein and was engaged in by the so-called Vienna Circle.[6] Logical Positivism, which was the Gospel of this school of thought, was characterized by a number of interrelated radical doctrines, the most basic of which was the "theory of meaning according to which the cognitive meaning of a sentence is its method of verification."[7]

1. Alfred Jules Ayer

The leading exponent of Logical Positivism in England was A.J. Ayer who presented the ideas of the Vienna Circle in his influential, uncompromisingly belligerent manifesto, *Language, Truth and Logic*.[8] The section

---

5 Ludwig Wittgenstein, *Lectures and Conversation on Aesthetics, Psychology and Religious Belief*, ed. by Cecil Barrett (Oxford: Basil Blackwell, 1966)

6 For a concise information about the Vienna Circle in relation to Wittgenstein, see F. Copleston, *Contemporary Philosophy* (London: Search Press, 1972), 5-7.

7 Morris Weitz, "Analysis, Philosophical" in the *Encyclopedia of Philosophy* 1st. ed., I, 102.

8 A.J. Ayer, *Language Truth and Logic* (London: Victor Gollancz, Ltd., 1951.)

of the book of interest here is the second part of the chapter VI, entitled
"Critique of Ethics and Theology", which is a typical example of the logical-positivistic treatment of the matter in question.

In this chapter, Ayer makes a paradigmatic analysis of religious statements of the creedal cognitive kind - the existence of God and life after death. He begins with the following syllogistic reasoning:

> If the existence of such a god (God of Christianity) were probable, then the proposition that he exists would be an empirical hypothesis. And in that case it would be possible to deduce from it, and other empirical hypothesis, certain experiential proposition which were not deducible from those other hypothesis alone. But in fact this is not possible. (p. 115)

The conclusion is for him so evident that he does not bother completing his syllogism but goes on to discuss the premisses. He dismisses shortly the cosmological argument for the existence of God and asserts rightly that the believer, when he says that God exists, means by it not merely that there is a requisite regularity in nature as some would tend to explain away the cosmological argument. The believer means rather, a transcendent Being who exists "who might be known through certain empirical manifestations but could not be defined in terms of these manifestations." (p. 115) But Ayer says in this case the word "God" would be a metaphysical term and being so the statement which uses it, i.e. "God exists" is metaphysical utterance which he has shown in the first chpter of his book to be neither true nor false but meaningless. He emphasizes the fact that this view is entirely different from the atheistic and the agnostic positions, because by the very same reason that it is meaningless to say "God exists", it, likewise, is meaningless to say "God does not exist". The agnostic's position is similarily invalid, because he still holds the proposition of either theist or atheist as meaningful, although he does not commit himself to any of them. According to Ayer, "... our view that all utterance about the nature of God are nonsensical, so far form being identical with, or even lending any support to either of these familiar contentions, is actually incompatible with them." (p. 115)

For Ayer therefore, the theistic, atheistic, and the agnostic positions are equally untenable. However, he offers the theist the consolation that although his assertions cannot possibly be true, they cannot be false either. It is only if he would claim that in asserting the existence of a transcendent God he is expressing a genuine proposition that Ayer feels entitled to disagree with him. The word "God" in this proposition may seem to refer to a real or possible entity corresponding to it, but when one enquires ionto the attributes of this entity, one discovers that "God in the usage is not a genuine name." (p. 116)

Ayer then moves on to treat the belief in an afterlife, which is conjoined to the belief in a transcendent God. In a single sentence, he finishes off this assertion thus:

> ... to say that there is something imperceptible inside a man which is his soul or his real self, and that it goes on living after he is dead, is to make a metaphysical assertion which has no more factual content than the assertion that there is a transcendent god. (p. 117)

2. Antony Flew

A more recent argument based on the same presuppositions and arriving at the same conclusion as Ayer's, but having some unique turns of its own, it is the one posed by Antony Flew in his book, *God and Philosophy*[9] and in his article in *New Essays in Philosophical Theology*.[10] A chapter of the latter book groups together five articles which deal with the now famous "University Discussion" on theology and falsification. Flew writes the introductory and concluding articles, from which one can glean his basic argument against theological statements, which he elaborates, applies or expands in his other works.

He begins with John Wisdom's parable in the heuristic article, "Gods"[11]. This much quoted article concerns two explorers who stumble into a clearing and are arguing whether there is or there is not a gardener who tends it. The theist is represented by the explorer who thinks that a gardener does tend it but he never shows himself. Flew shows that in trying to differentiate this "invisible gardener" from ordinary gardeners, the explorer ends up by qualifying the assertion to some other expression of a different status and finally the statement is "killed by inches"; it dies the death by a thousand qualifications. (p. 97) This, he then goes

---

9 A. Flew, *God and Philosophy* (London: Hutchinson Press, 1966).

10 A. Flew and A. MacIntyre, eds. *New Essays in Philosophical Theology* (London: SCM Press, 1969).

11 John Wisdom, "Gods" in *Logic and Language* (Oxford: University Press, 1955), 186-206.

on to say, is the peculiar danger of creedal utterances such as "God has a plan", "God created the world", "God loves us as a father loves his children." He points out, and rightly so, that although in themselves these statements are not necessarily assertive statements, believers do intend them to be assertions. But assert that "such and such is the case" is necessarily equivalent to denying that "such and such is *not* the case." Here is where Flew deviates from Ayer. Having had the advantage of a historical perspective and of seeing the Verification Priciple under fire and suffering a similar agony of dying the death of even more than a thousand qualifications, he chooses falsification as his criterion for the meaningfulness of propositions. So instead of asking, as Ayer does, for experiential propositions that could be deduced from the theological proposition, Flew demands that propositions possibly counting against the assertion or incompatible with its truth be given. He argues thus:

> For if the utterance is indeed an assertion, it will necessarily be an equivalent to a denial of the negation of that assertion. And anything which could count against the assertion, or which could induce the speaker to withdraw it and to admit that it had been mistaken, must be part of (or the whole of) the meaning of the negation of that assertion. And to know the meaning of the negation of an assertion, is as near as makes no matter, to know the meaning of that assertion. And if there is nothing which a putative assertion denies, then there is nothing which it asserts either and so it is not really an assertion. (p. 98)

Being himself convinced that the theological utterances are rendered meaningless by such an argument, he nevertheless challenges the Symposiats with the question: "What would have to occur or to have occured to constitute for a disproof of the love of or of the existence of God?" (p. 99)

His concluding article which comes after other contributions, claims that the theologian, when relentlessly pursued about his assertions, would resort to qualification. (p. 107) He also insisted, against some reductionistic interpretations, on the assertive character of religious statements. Against Hare's "Blick" explanation[12] of theological utterance, Flew justifiably but pointedly and not without malice, asks rhetorically: " If Hare's religion really is a "Blick" involving no cosmological assertions about value and activities of a supposed personal creator, then surely

---

12 This is treated in a separate discussion of Hare in the next section, "Non-Cognitive Treatment of Creedal Statements", p. 17

he is not a Christian at all?" (p. 108)

Finally, he suggests that perhaps the philosophers of religion resort to "doublethink"[13] to retain their faith in a loving God in face of the reality of the heartless and indifferent world.

3. Appraisal

Much water has passed under the bridge since Ayer wrote his *Language, Truth and Logic*. The developments in the history of linguistic analysis, particularly the publication of Wittgenstein's *Philosophical Investigations*, have gone a long way to soften the intransigence of the logical-positivistic criterion of meaning. With it goes much of the sting of both Ayer's and Flew's critiques of religious language. The logical-positivistic presupposition has been shown to limit itself to the empirical world which does not exhaust reality as experienced by man. The verificational theory of meaning with all its subsequent modification have likewise been shown to be inadequate and in fact itself unverifiable. Moreover, the treatment of religious statements incorrectly took these statements as ordinary empirical statements without paying attention to their creedal aspect.

To the credit of the logical positivists, however, must be counted the fact that they did show a good grasp of the question at the stake. Ayer, Flew and other adherents of their thoughts all insisted on the cognitive intention of the believer's assertions. They were scrupulous in allowing nothing to cloud the issue. Ayer saw correctly that the creedal statements on the existence of God did not simply mean a statement about the regularity of nature. Flew insisted rightly that to interpret these assertions as "crypto-commands, expressions of wishes, disguised ejaculations, concealed ethics"[14] would make them neither orthodox nor effective, at least, we must add however, if they were excusively so interpreted. In their analyses, these philosophers naturally tried to show that the believer's assertions were in fact neither assertions nor were they in fact cognitive, but the point is that they did recognize that these statements were meant

---

13 "Doublethink" means the power of holding two contradictory beliefs simultaneously and accepting both of them. The party intellectually knows reality, but by the exercise of doublethink he also satisfies himself that reality is not involved - George Orwell, cited in A. Flew and MacIntyre, *New Essays in Philosophical Theology*, 108

14 *Ibid.*, 98.

to be cognitive assertions. Furthermore, they brought to attention the important point that in the analysis of religious language the concern is with meaning and not with the truth or falsity of the assertion. It does not follow that therefore one is not in any sense concerned with existence but only with language. Only, that before going on to investigate further, there is need for an initial linguistic clarity.

III. *Non-Cognitive Treatment of Creedal Statements*

Faced by the challenge of the logical positivistic analysis of religious language, a number of contemporary philosophers, impressed by the difficuty of showing that religious statements are factual in the sense of being open to experiential verification or falsification and yet not willing to accept the conclusion that they are meaningless, have evolved non-cognitive theories about religious language. The adjective "non-cognitive" is used here to designate the type of analysis which focuses on the "attitudinal" aspect of creedal statements. These analysts see functions of religious language other than that of making some kind of factual assertions. They re-interpret these statements and come to the conclusion that although they are neither true nor false, they nevertheless are meaningful, because they declare a certain attitude towards life, the world, or one's relationship with one's fellowman.

1. John Wisdom

John Wisdom's subtle and thought-provoking essay "Gods" begins the series of the non-cognitive accounts of religious language. In this article Wisdom rephrases the expression "belief in God" into the question: "Is the belief in gods reasonable?" This, he says, may be further resolved into the following components: (1) Is there ever any behaviour which gives reason to believe in any sort of mind? (2) Are there mind patterns in nature beside the human and animal patterns and can these other mind patterns be superhuman? (3) Are we justified in calling these mind patterns manifestations of a divine being?

By means of illuminating examples, he points out that it is possible to have befor one's eyes all the items of a pattern and still to miss the pattern. Likewise, the expression "There is a God" although it conveys an attitude to the familiar, also "evinces some recognition of pattern in time easily missed and that, therefore, difference as to there being any gods or not is in part a difference as to what is so, and therefore as to the facts, though not in the simple ways which first occurred to us." (p. 192) "Facts" as used here is better expressed as "configuration of facts".[15]

Wisdom makes another approach by his now famous parable of the two explorers arguing about the existence of a gardener tending a garden in a forest clearing - the same parable which Antony Flew used in his analysis. The two man proceed in an experimental way to support their arguments about the existence or non-existence of a gardener, by examining the garden carefully and other neglected gardens. After arriving at the knowledge of the same facts about neglected gardens in general and about this particular one, both continue to persist in their contentions. Wisdom points out, the meaning of the parable thus:

> The one says a gardener comes unseen and unheard. He is manifested only in his works... The other says "There is no gardener" and with this difference in what they say about the gardener goes a difference in how they feel towards the garden, in spite of the fact that neither expects anything of it which the other does not expect. (p. 193)

Applying the parable to the theistic issue, Wisdom continues: "The difference as to whether a God exists involves our feeling more than most scientific disputes and in this respect is more like a difference as to whether there is a beauty in a thing." (p. 421) He therefore suggests that the settling of the theistic issue should follow the method of settling the difference as to whether or not there is beauty in a thing.

The theistic position is then elaborated as the projection of human emotions of awe, of confidence, of unease beneath the all-seeing Eye, of guilt, of vengeance, of hate, of serenity, etc. With the advance of knowledge, some of these projections have been given up or the words expressing them have been given a new meaning. In short, the difference between the theistic and atheistic position is primarily interpreted as largely a "difference of emotional attitude in the face of the world,"[16] which makes a difference in the perception of patterns of the same fact seen.

---

15 J. Macquarrie, *God Talk* (London: SCM Press, 1967), 115

16 *Loc. Cit.*

2. Richard Hare

Another representative of the non-cognitive analysis of theistic statements is Richard M. Hare. In his contribution as a symposiast to the "University Discussion", he treats the theistic issue by means of a parable of his own - the parable of the lunatic, who is convinced that all dons want to murder him. No amount of argument can convince him of the contrary. He explains all the actions of dons according to his first psychological attitude which Hare baptizes with the term "Blick". He then asserts that not only the lunatic has a "Blick"; each one has his own "Blick" about things, the only difference being that the sane man has a sane "Blick", while the lunatic has an insane one. Hare refers to Hume and paraphrases him as saying that "our whole commerce with the world depends upon our 'Blick' about the world; and that difference between 'Blick' about the world cannot be settled by observation of what happens in the world." (p. 101) He considers as a mistake the position of those who treat theistic statements as a sort of scientific explanation. These statements constitute rather the "Blick" by which one decides what is and what is not an explanation. The practical consequences in one's actions drawn from this "Blick" spell the difference between those who *really* believe in God and those who really disbelieve in him. He emphasizes the word "really", because he thinks that there are people who think they have given up their religion when they discard its external expressions, but in reality they retain their religious "Blick".

Hare distinguishes his parable from that of Wisdom by pointing out the element of concern in the lunatic which is not in the two men arguing about the gardener. By this, Hare seems to distinguish the religious "Blick" from other "Blicken" by what might be called its existential importance. The two men were engaging in a theoretical discussion whereas the lunatic was frightfully concerned about the safety of his live.

3. R.F. Holland

Another interpretation of religious talk is given by R.F. Holland in his article "Religious Discourse and Theological Discourse"[17] where he

---

[17] R.F. Holland, "Religious Discourse and Theological Discourse" in *Australasian Journal of Philosophy*, XXXIV (December, 1956), 147-163.

reduces this talk to a language of worship. He distinguishes first of all religious discourses from theological discourses as talking to God, from talking about God. Theological discourses, he claims, can either be theistic or anti-theistic. Somewhat allergic to theological discourse, he refuses to class theistic theological discourses with religious talk.

Doing little justice to theology and curiously taking C.S. Lewis and G. Pappini as his representative theologians, Holland asserts that theological discourse, because it speaks *about* God is bound to talk about him in either a quasi-scientific or quasi-atheistic way. He groups as quasi-scientific discourse "all those discussions which are marked by a preoccupation with the existence of God and hence by speculations as to where or when God might exist and what sort of an existence God might have." (p. 154) To the second, he includes those "discussions in which it is supposed that God can be discovered or met with directly in a special experience called religious experience." (p. 157)

Religious talk in contrast to the foregoing, Holland asserts, does not talk *about* God but *to* him. This does not mean that the word "God" would appear only in the vocative or in the second person statements in religious discourse. Religious people do reflect and meditate. But their statements that on the surface may appear as talk about are "statements which function, so to speak, as the high-level generelization of religious expression, summarizing the believer's attitude to his existence and focusing it directly into an attitude of worship." (p. 149) They are much more statements about the speaker or more exactly about the believer's relationship to God. Thus the believer's statements like "God is creator to whom one owes everything" or "God is the God of mercy of whose forgiveness one stands in need" are statements about the speaker more than about God. The believer, experiencing goodness and beauty in his life sees it as a gift from God. Overwhelmed with gratitude, he expresses his loving dependence on the Giver of gifts.

Knowledge of God in religious discourse, Holland claims, is *not* synonymous with knowledge that God exists. It doesn't even include it. He writes:

> The idea of God's existence may enter into religious discourse when a religious person asserts that God exists as a way of affirming his religiuos belief, his belief in God. But if in making his assertion he takes himself to be saying not simply *that* he believes in God, but what he believes in regard to God (i.e. that God is a being who exists) then I think he passes at once from religious discourse *about* God, and in a quasi-scientific manner. (p. 160)

"There is not", he goes on more radically, "even a possibility of cognitive encounter with the object of faith." (p. 161) He thinks, in fact, that God's existence as a factual hypothesis is not needed in religious belief. On the contrary it is detrimental to it, because "it would involve a cessation of faith, since it would replace it by a take-it-or-leave-it acceptance of fact." (p. 161) To have religious faith in a fact is a contradiction or even a downright idolatry.

The necessity of God, he continues, is not the necessity that he should be a fact, but that he should be what he is, i.e. should possess *in aeternum* the properties ascribable to him. In statements like "God is good" and "God is merciful" the qualities are so attributed as to preclude them from being predicated of any existent being, because one attributes them in an absolute way. These statements are rather the expressions of gratitude of one who is grateful for his existence and realizes that he owes it to God. Finally, the statement concerning God as creator, Holland explains as more like saying, "I do not owe my existence to myself." Religious language is thus for Holland a humble acceptance of the believer of his contingent existance which expresses itself in an attitude of worship.

4. R.B. Braithwaite

A much discussed reductionistic approach to religious language is R.B. Braithwaite's "An Empiricist's View of the Nature of Religious Belief."[18] In this article, religious statements are interpreted as moral assertions. To the challenge of the logical positivists, that religious statements do not have the kind of meaning attributed to statements of empirical facts, he responds by agreeing with them. However, according to him, religious statements have a use and in this sense have a meaning. A religious assertion, he says, is used primarily as a moral assertion. It is "the intention... to act in a particular sort of way specified in the assertion." (p. 237) Specifically, it is a "declaration of adherence to a policy of action, a declaration of commitment to a way of life." (p. 239) Thus the

---

18 R.B. Braithwaite, "An Empiricist's View of the Nature of Religious Belief" in John Hick (ed.) *The Existence of God* (New York: Macmillan Co., 1964), 229-252.

intention of a Christian to follow the Christian way of life is not merely a criterion for the sincerity of his belief in the assertions of Christianity; it is the very criterion for the *meaningfulness* of his assertion.

He then points out some ways in which a religious assertion differs from the specifically moral assertion. One difference is the lack of explicitation in religious assertions regarding the specific policy of conduct which the believer intends to pursue. But how can one intend an unspecified policy? Braithwaite solves this difficulty thus:

> If a religious assertion is regarded as representative of a large number of assertions of the same religious system, the body of assertions of which the particular one is a representative specimen is taken by the asserter as implicitly specifying a particular way of life. (p. 240)

This assimilation of religious assertions into moral resolutions blurs the boundary lines between the different religions and in fact between religion and, let us say, philanthropism. Braithwaite recognizes the first difficulty and develops a theory that the differences between religions lie in the set of stories associated with each. This brings in a propositional element to religious assertions lacking in the purely moral assertion. But it is not necessary, according to Braithwaite, that the asserter believe in the truth of the stories involved in the assertions. What is necessary is that the story should be understood as having a meaning. The function of these stories is to make it psychologically easier for the believer to resolve upon and carry through a course of action which might be contrary to his inclination.[19]

To summarize: Braithwaite regards religious assertions as "the assertion of an intention to carry out a certain behaviour policy, subsumable under a sufficiently general principle to be a moral one, together with the implicit or explicit statement but not the assertion of certain stories." (p. 251) This view, he believes, does justice to both the empiricists' demand that meaning must be regulated to empirical use as well as to the religious man's claim that his beliefs are to be taken seriously.

---

19 This view of the Gospel stories as "noble motives for moral conduct" was a common view in the period of the Enlightment! See, for example, Lessing, *Die Erziehung des Menschengeschlechts*. Further on, Kant would consider religious truths mainly as postulates of the moral law. Cf. Immanuel Kant, *Kritik der praktischen Vernunft*.

5. Appraisal

The appraisal of the non-cognitive treatment of religious language must state from the outset that if taken exclusively and uncritically, such a non-cognitive view would prove most fatal not only for theology but also for religion, because the reinterpretation of religious language is at least a misinterpretation if not a downright dissolution of what is essential to it, namely its truth claims. Having taken a fence-sitter's position, such an analysis has succeeded only in courting protests from both sides of the fence. From the logical positivists' camp represented by Antony Flew, comes justified critique that such an analysis clouds the issue and on the side of theologians and philosophers of religion are heard expressions of disappointment and reproach at its poor showing in representing the believer's position.[20]

It must however be acknowledged that this type of analysis has put forward an important point, namely, that there are indeed non-cognitive aspects of religious language. Wisdom and Hare are quite right in saying that religious belief has the character of a *Weltanschauung*. And certainly much of religious language is talking *to* God, rather than just talking about him, as Holland insists. Braithwaite likewise points out an important test of true religiosity, namely, personal commitment to a way of life.

The predicament of the above-mentioned analysts may be taken as an example of a philosophical blind alley. As Boyce Gibson aptly puts it, they have swerved from the very legitimate statement, "Religion does not consist in making statements" to the quite different and incorrect statement, "Religion has nothing to do with making statements."[21] From the correct obsrevation that theistic conviction without personal commitment cannot characterize a believer, they did not go further to see that neither does personal involvement without theistic conviction.

The reason for getting into such a blind alley is the fact that these philosophers did not think of questioning the empiristic premisses with

---

20 These philosophers and theologians would react to the reductionistic analysts by making their own analysis of religious propositions re-emphasizing the cognitive aspects of these statements. Cf. pp. 22-29 of his work.

21 Boyce-Gibson, "Modern Philosophers Consider Religion" in *Australasian Journal of Philosophy* XXXV (December, 1957), 174.

which they started. From these premisses, however, the only kind of religion that would be acceptable is one which is "detached from the world and unresponsive to intelligence,"[22] which cannot claim as religion must claim, the whole loyalty of man. Boyce-Gibson indicates a way out of the blind alley, namely, by backing up to the starting point: "Those who wish to dissent from their (logical positivists') conclusions are committed to disputing their premisses."[23]

IV. *The Cognitive Treatment of Creedal Statements*

The non-cognitive interpretation of religious language was understandably regarded by a number of theologians and philosophers of religion as a misinterpretation if not a betayal of the believer's position. They felt that this type of analysis was a side-stepping of the problems involved in the theistic issue. Granting that the Christian way of life, as constituted by human activity, involves more than simply believing certain propositions about matters such as the existence of God, creation, last judgement, etc., they nevertheless insisted that it does involve believing in these claims and this belief is presupposed by the activities of Christians. Urged by the desire to vindicate religious language, which, in their opinion, was watered down by the analysts previously treated, these philosophers would develop their own theories about religious language with a decided stress on its cognitive aspects.

1. I.M. Crombie

Coming out as one of the first protests against the non-cognitive analysis of theological statements was a collection of essays edited by Basil Mitchell entitled *Faith and Logic*.[24] The second article in this book is I.M. Crombie's "The Possibility of Theological Statements". (pp. 32-83) The introduction at once makes a straightforward declaration that factual beliefs are fundamental to Christianity and that the expression of these beliefs, which he refers to as "the making of theological statements" is possible.

---

22 *Ibid.*, 184.

23 *Ibid.*, 185.

24 Basil Mitchell, *Faith and Logic* (London: Allen and Unwin, 1957).

The rest of the article is devoted to the question: How are theological statements possible? The problem lies, he says, in the fact that in theological statements, there is a sense in which we cannot know exactly what they are about nor what it is they assert, as for example when one says, "God is jealous", or "There are three Persons in one God", etc. He indicates a possible solution of the problem as consisting in "defining the sense in which... we can know enough of these things for our speech about them to have an intelligible use." (p. 35) He proposes to do this by first summarizing the position of the critic of theological statements and then answering his objections.

The critic's position according to Crombie may be condensed to two points: (1) Theological statements form a system without reference to anything in the real world, and (2) The subject of theological statements (God) is an elusive concept which causes the statements to go around in a circular maze. Crombie sets out to answer this by: (1) partially delineating the subject matter of theological statements, and (2) fixing the reference range within which this subject is to be located.

Crombie expresses no objection to the critic's position if it means merely that there is no region of experience which one can point out to say: "That is what theological statements are about!" But Crombie maintains that this does not show that theological statements have no legitimate use. He admits that in theological statements with "God" as subject, there is an element of elusiveness. The use "God" in these statements is that of an "improper proper name", because even if it is used as a proper name having a referent, it does not have the common properties of a proper name such as definitely designating its referent. The predicates are likewise used in an unusual sense. This paradoxical feature of theological statements need not, however, be regarded as demonstrating the meaninglessness of such statements but rather "contributing to a grasp of their meaning by a partial characterization of their subject." (p. 34) This partial characterization of the subject may be summarized thus: There exists an object of discourse which is particular but not indicable and that this is "neither similar to nor in normal relation with any spatio-temporal object." (p. 150) This step is meant to draw the attention away from all irrelevant subjects.

A further step is the fixing of the reference range in which this object of theological discourse is to be more or less located. Granted that "God" as this subject, is an indicating word, how does it supply a warrant for religious belief? What space-time world, persons or event impel one to connect the divine region to our world? Crombie answers: Christ. And more fully:

> Christ provides the answer to his (critic's) challenge that we have no right to claim that there exists a being corresponding to the conception of God, for we ascribe to Christ divine origin and He also provides the answer to the problem how we know what to say about God, for He is the image or a declaration of God to us. (p. 69)

Due to the unique nature of the subject of theological statements which makes it inappropriate to talk about him in a way one talks about spatio-temporal beings, these statements must be conceived in a way one conceives parables, i.e. as stories which are not to be literally taken but as faithful expressions of an underlying reality, the point of the parable being the resemblance between the truth expressed and the story which expresses it. It is in this way, according to Crombie, "that theological statements acquire fixed meanings." (p. 71)

In his arguments, Crombie used the following hypothesis: (1) that there can be good grounds for committing category-transgressions (which he had to do in applying predicating qualities proper to spatio-temporal creatures to the unique subject of theological statements); (2) that there can be meanings which do not correspond to clear and distinct ideas (which is the meaning Crombie attached to the subject matter of the statements in question, of whom one can have no clear and distinct ideas but only imperfect analogical ones); and (3) that the criterion for the meaningfulness of statements lies in the legitimate use to which they can be put. He then concludes:

> Having given a reference range for theological statements and said how they are to be taken... we are justified in claiming that they are meaningful. For, in order that an utterance be meaningful, what more is necessary than that speaker and hearer know or can find out what it is being made about and how to determine the extent of the claim which is being made about it? (p. 83)

2. John Hick

Another philosopher of religion who expressed dissatisfaction with the non-cognitive interpretations of creedal statements is John Hick. In his book, *Faith and Knowledge*[25], he devotes some enlightening chapters to an epistemological theory and structure in which religious faith can justifiably claim a cognitive aspect. The core of this theory is the statement that "all awareness of environment is awareness of it as significant."[26] This means that to know this or that object is to apprehend the environment in which it is found to be significant in this or that way. Religious faith shares this common epistemological structure with cognition as such. Religious language is not irrational. To "Know God by faith" is a recognition of significance that is not a pure automatic reflex but an exercise of intelligence. What makes religious faith unique is its being a *total* interpretation of things. But this is not just a way of looking at the world. For Hick, what goes over and above this interpretation is what is most distinctive in religion, namely, its ontological claim that besides the world thus interpreted, there is an extra person we call God. In Hick's words:

> It (religious belief) thus entails an ontological claim which has no analogy in the sphere of aesthetics... Theistic religion in claiming that the world mediates a divine activity, must also claim that God exists as a real Being, transcending our world as well as meeting us in and through it. This ontological claim is the final point of distinction not only between religion and aesthetics but also between religion and ethics... For the theist the word "God" does not designate a logical construction nor is it simply a poetic term for the world as a whole, it refers to the unique transcendent personal creator of the universe.(p. 20)

In another article, Hick further claims that theological statements are verifiable - naturally not in the logical-positivistic sense, but in the sense of the possibility of ascertaining their truth by the removal of grounds for rational doubts.[27] But even if this could be done, Hick admits that he was not making an absolute justification of theism. His way of verification is capable of theistic and atheistic applications. And the condition is: human personal freedom. Hick explains: "Whether the theistic claim is justified... is question for each individual exercising

---

25 John Hick, *Faith and Knowledge* (New York: Cornell University Press, 1969).

26 *Ibid.*, 20

27 Cf. John Hick, "Theology and Verification" in *Theology Today*, 17 (1960) 15-17.

his cognitive power in relation to the environment in which he finds himself and responding in his personal freedom and responding to its claims and calls." (p. 146)

3. John Macquarrie

Among those who insist on the cognitive aspect of creedal statements, there are those who expressedly rely on metaphysical-ontological arguments to explain religious language. The chief metaphysical options are some forms of Thomism, personal idealism, process philosophy and existentialism.

John Macquarrie, recognizing the challenge of linguistic analysis and yet aware that the days of iconoclastic logical positivism are over, offers another interpretation of religious language in his book, *God-Talk*[28]. His main contention is that the problem of religious language has its roots in the gap between finite reality and God and that a possible solution is to provide an adequate logical bridge to fill the gap, which for him consists in the "language of being".[29]

In the first part of the book, Macquarrie surveys the contemporary approaches to theological talk. In his treatment of the analysis of the religious statements in the line of the contemporary British analytic philosophy, he considers many points raised by the non-cognitive analysts "of great interest", but he declares quite clearly: "... my own conviction is that any satisfactory account of religious language (and still more of theological language) must ascribe to it a definately cognitive dimension and take seriously its claims to deal with the knowledge of God." (p. 110) He realizes that theological talk is quite different from other ways of speaking, but he insists: " This does not mean that it is to be lumped with emotive utterance or that it is to be denied genuine cognitive insight, though the theologian may reasonably be expected to show on what grounds the claims of this language are based." (p. 89)

His approach to religious language makes use of existential philosophy, because it is his basic conviction that "any adequate analysis of religious language must be concerned with existential analysis." (p. 119) In the last chapter of the book he develops the theme which actually runs

---

28 John Macquarrie, *God-Talk: An Examination of the Language and Logic of Theology* (London: SCM Press, 1967).

29 *Ibid.*, 238.

through the previous chapters, namely, that the logic of theology tends to express itself in terms of existence and being and therefore that theological language must be "an existential-ontological language." (p. 238)

Roughly speaking, his thesis has two parts: The first consists in a phenomenological analysis of the triadic (speaker-subject matter-hearer) relationship in which speaking takes place. The same relations hold good for theological speaking. Language is thus a means of bringing some features of the shared world to light. It may be used in different ways simultaneously in the same discourse situation. Similarly, theological discourse makes use of several modes of speaking: existential, ontological, mythical, metaphysical, and empirical. These modes are used correlatively for mutual clarification. As theology becomes more and more reflective, there appears the need for a second phase, namely, its language would have to posit an analogy between the being of finite reality and God's being. Here is where Macquarrie draws on Heidegger. He considers Heidegger's analysis of the distinction between Being and beings such as to allow the Christian to identify Being with God. He sees in Heidegger's ontology an adequate account of the analogical relation between God and the world.

In this venture of making an existential analysis of God-talk, Macquarrie realizes the relevance of logical analysis especially in its insight that it is important to examine language in the concrete situation in which it occurs. He thinks that it is in this connection that linguistic analysis impinges on existential analysis and he believes that together these could provide the foundations for an adequate and contemporary philosophical theology.

4. E.L. Mascall

Another attempt to provide a rational justification for religious language is E.L. Mascall's *Words and Images*[30] which resorts to Thomistic principles for the task.

The first section of the book is devoted to the critique of the logical-positivistic and non-cognitive treatments of religious language. He points out as the fundamental weakness of these positions the uncri-

---

30 E.L. Mascall, *Words and Images: A Study in Theological Discourse* (New York: Longmans, Green and Co. Ltd., 1957).

tical epistemological assumption "that perception is essentially identical with sensation, as a result of which our knowledge of the world was arbitrarily blocked at the level of sensible phenomenon." (p. 170) Against this view, he argues in a thomistic fashion that perception[31] is primarily an intellectual act in which the mind passes through it to grasp concrete reality. For him, this concrete reality has a transensible intelligible nature. This view of perception explains how the mind gets to know physical objects and other persons and opens the possibility of knowing God as Mascall shows in the following:

> My contention then is that we have a whole range of knowledge, knowledge not but through sensible phenomena, which is essentially obscure and opaque; it includes in its scope some of the most important aspects of our experience such as our knowledge of physical objects, other persons and God... Our knowledge of God, like our knowledge of physical objects while obscure and opaque is genuine knowledge. It is partial, inchoate, and subject to error, but it is not incurably fallacious, for the mind though fallible is self-correcting. (p. 75 f.)

The cognitive process for Mascall involves commitment, contemplation and penetration beneath the level of the phenomenon. Only such a contemplative penetration can apprehend a transensible entity which confronts the human mind as a mystery. As one penetrates into this mystery, the range and clarity of vision progressively increases, but likewise the vast background of darkness which surrounds the small central area of which one has a relatively clear vision. Though remaining obscure, the mystery illuminates other things.

Applying this to Christian belief, Mascall indirectly criticizes the non-cognitive analysts when he asserts:

> The Christian does not simply give intellectual assent to the proposition "God is love" and then, when confronted with hostile evidence glibly redefine his terms so that the proposition will still be true. He gets to know God better and better the longer he lives in the world and comes more and more to know as a matter of personal experience how very profound and ponderable a thing the love of God is. (p. 83)

Having established the epistemological foundation of the knowledge of God, Mascall tackles the question of the possibility of talking about God.

---

[31] Mascall uses the word "perception" with a special nuance which goes beyond the ordinary philosophical use of the term. His aim is to link sensation as much as possible with intellectual cognition.

Corresponding to the epistemological principle of perception explained above, he similarly asserts that linguistic formulae, "are neither *objecta quae* of communication... nor are they merely more or less accurate structural replicas of the thought which has been coded into them, but they are *objecta quibus* - means through which two minds are enabled to enter into the sharing of a common intellectual life." (p. 92)

There still remains the question: How can we use words which signify objects of sensation to talk about God who has nothing in common with the objects of sensation? To answer this question, Mascall resorts to the traditional principle of analogy. One can talk analogically about God, because there is a certain affinity between God and finite beings in spite of the radical difference in their existential status. In Mascall's words: "It is because finite beings participate in the perfection of their creator and stand in a perpetual relation of dependence upon him as the source from which the existence is derived, that one and the same concept or image can refer to the creator and to his creature in different analogical words." (p. 108)

This brings the image factor in Mascall's theory. According to him, there are aspects of reality which can be reached only by meditation of images and this applies most especially to the divine reality. Having thus rounded up his argument, he concludes:

> My hope as I come to the end of my argument is that I have done something to show that the discourse of Christian theology and religion is neither psittacistic nonsense nor disguised pep-talk but is rational conversation of a unique type which has its own peculiar method and discipline. (p. 122)

5. Appraisal

It is clear from the above discussion that the analysts just discussed vary in approach and method and are one mainly in their insistence on the cognitive character and meaningfulness of theological assertions. In their insistence on the real character of the theistic claim and their refusal to water down the concept "God", they share the following commendation:

> ... there are religious thinkers who have appreciated anew, and with much discernment, the "beyondness" or transcendence of God and who have found in the new philosophical moves a way of exhibiting the apparently incomprehensible character of essential religious claims and the pitfalls which beset the attempt to

make them comprehensible in terms of what is sometimes described as a crude theism, and here the new philosophy has certainly something to say which religious persons should heed.[32]

The effectiveness of each approach must, however, be appraised separately. Crombie's endeavor to fix the reference range for the subject of theological talk is valuable in pulling the attention away from philosophical blind alleys. His suggestion that there may be good grounds for committing category transgressions intentionally to make a point is refreshingly bold and opens the way for the possibility of what Ramsey calls "odd language"[33] in talking about God, who is not to be spoken of in the ordinary way since he cannot be fixed into any category. John Hick and E. Mascall approached the question of creedal statements in an epistemological way - Hick, with his "theory of significance" and Mascall with his "intellectual perception". For those who set out to establish the cognitive character of theological statements, the question of epistemology is bound to come up. To begin with empiristic epistemological principles would inevitably lead to logical-positivistic conclusions about the nature of knowledge and hence about the character of creedal statements. Hence such theories as Hick's and Mascall's are to be seen as real contributions to the clarification of religious language . As a reviewer of Mascall's book writes: "The author is to be commended on the relevance of epistemological considerations to the analysis of theological statements."[34] Of the two, Hick's "total interpretation" is more original, but Mascall's elaboration and up-dating of the thomistic principle of perception seem to be more coherent. John Macquarrie's existential approach to the problem is to be commended, because every mature consideration of religious language must ultimately confront the semantis aspects of words. It must treat the questions of being, man's existence, history. According to a reviewer of Macquarrie's book, by approaching the problem as Macquarrie does, we can avoid three pitfalls: "making the human word divine, making

---

32 H.D. Lewis,"Contemporary Empiricism and the Philosophy of Religion" in *Philosophy*, XXXII (July, 1957), 410.

33 For a more detailed explanation of "odd language", see I.T. Ramsey, *Christian Discourse: Some Logical Exploration* (London: Oxford University Press, 1965).

34 W. Alston, "*Words and Images*" by Mascall - "A Review" in *The Philosophical Review*, LXIII (1959), 410

the divine word of self-communication to us impossible, confusing the affirmation of faith in God with the human verbalization of 'God acting'".[35]

It is, however, necessary to express a certain reservation about Macquarrie's emphasis on Heidegger. If done critically and selectively, an application of heideggerian philosophy to the whole problematic can be of much value, but if one allows oneself to be fascinated by the linguistic adventures of the later Heidegger, such a reception can prove detrimental to theology. It is likewise fatal to succumb to the temptation of identifying Heidegger's "Being" with God.

On the whole, the group of philosophers treated in this section may be considered to have begun constructively to use linguistic analysis in the problem of religious language in spite of their still in times too metaphysical approach and terminology. Here and there and especially in their original impulse, there may be still apologetic tinges to be detected. There is however a decided moving away from polemics and an opening up to a fruitful dialogue between linguistic analysis and theology.

V. *Functional-Situational Approach To Creedal Statements*

The term functional-situational approach which is coined by the writer is here meant the kind of analysis of religious statements inspired by the insights of the later Wittgenstein. Philosophers who engage in this type of analysis do not make global theories. There is less of theorizing and more of "looking and seeing" when the engine of language is not idling. There is a search for the "depth grammar" in which one encounters the real significance of words and sentences which may not be shown by the "surface grammar".[36] These analysts aim at achieving clarity not by logical or mathematical reduction but by appeal to the diversity of ways in which things are and can be said, and by patient probing into the roots of religious discourse displaying constructively its various features as it is actually used and lived.

---

35 T. O'Meara, "Outlining the Problem" in *Continuum*, V (Autumn, 1967), 586.

36 The difference between "depth" and "surface" grammars is explained in Chapter II of this work, p.44.

1. Dallas High

To be numbered among the pioneer works in this type of analysis is Dallas High's book, *Language, Persons and Belief*[37]. In a truly Wittgensteinian fashion, High devotes the first chapter of the second part of his book to "seeing and looking" at one actual religious use of language, namely, belief utterance.

First he shows that such belief utterances have a "family resemblance" to other belief utterances of all kinds woven throughout the fabric of human discourses. He thus locates them in a "form of life" - human life, with its extra-linguistic connotations. He then proceeds to enumerate the uses of the verb "believe" giving examples of how each is used both in everyday speech and in religious talk, showing that the word is used to designate not a mere passive behavioral or mental disposition but that it is also an active, intentional performative utterance.

High takes pains to show the significant difference between the first person indicative use of beliefs and the second and the third person uses. The first person use has a decisive performative character as distinct from the reporting or observing character of the other two uses. First person belief statements stand therefore on a different logical ground from other belief statements. He establishes a definite connection between "first person believing", "persons" and "personal backing" on the one hand and "religious acts of believing" on the other. From this, he draws the claim that creedal statements do not immediately concern themselves with question of facts, of descriptions, or of objects. They are rather "self-involving questions like the relation, loyalty, trust or value I may place in another person or something personalized."[38]

High holds that in seeing belief talk as a part of the human condition of language and persons, one avoids the misuse of this kind of talk as exemplified by the language of fideism which is theological talk insulated from the ordinary intelligent human personal language. In contrast to this position which considers faith as self-justifying, High suggests that "justification" and "reasons" are to be given, but these are to be given by "persons" and not by rules, logical or otherwise. This anchoring of

---

37 Dallas High, *Language, Persons and Belief* (New York: Oxford University Press, 1969).

38 *Ibid.*, 176

belief takes many forms: empirical, authorative, historical, all of which are woven and interconnected into all spheres of ordinary life. Thus religious believing becomes a sharing in the human adventure.

2. William Hordern

Another attempt to bring theological language into a conversation with analytical philosophy inspired by the later Wittgenstein is William Hordern's *Speaking of God*.[39] It begins with a clear historical and critical study of analytical philosophy and of linguistic analysis of theological language so far made. He then adopts W. Zuurdeeg's concept of "convictional language,"[40] for his analysis. In kernel, the approach holds that religion has within itself the ability to persuade through the use of reason and within the limits of a person's framework of convictions. The function of analysis is to detect the conviction hidden in theological language.

Hordern holds that theology has its own language game. It has a particular use related to man's religious life, worship and commitment. It has its own vocabulary, definable only in terms of one another and it has its own means of verification based upon its convictional basis. However, this uniqueness in no way isolates theology from the rest of life. But how can a non-believer learn this language game? Hordern answers: "The Christian must share with the non-believer the way of life from which theological language comes." Therefore:"There is no way to analyze the language game of Christian theology without analyzing the Christian way of life." (p. 190) He thus goes on to treat the context of theological language - the Christian Community.

Theological language is a language of a community of faith, and by faith he means "the response of the whole man, who having been convicted

---

39 W. Hordern,*Speaking of God* (New York: Macmillan Co., Inc., 1967).

40 Cf. W. Zuurdeeg, *An Analytical Philosophy of Religion* (New York: Abingdon Press, 1958). Zuurdeeg uses the word "conviction" to mean all persuasions concerning the meaning and significance of life whether good or bad, god or devils, ideals, and so forth. Convictions are sufficient grounds of action, from which flow decisions which govern life. "Convictional language" applied to religious language brings out the fact that the man who speaks of his God, is not describing how he feels but is pointing to that which has "convicted" him. What the conviction is, cannot be a matter of personal taste but depends on the nature of his "convictor." The "convictor" is that which has power to overwhelm and overcome, which can draw irresistibly. The convictor is usually presented by the "witness" of those who have been convicted. A man who is "convicted" undergoes a radical change. He is "converted."

by a convictor commits himself in trust." (p. 104) These convictions involved in religious language are unique in that they are ultimate convictions of a man's life, by which he lives and dies. One of the factors that convict the believer is the experience of the mysterious. Religious language is rooted in the realm of mystery and the clue to this mystery is Jesus Christ who is the ultimate Convictor and who therefore sets the terms of the discourse. The proper language of mystery is the language of worship. In Hordern's words: " Although theology deals with problems, it is never primarily problem solving venture; it is the servant of the worshipping community. When theology forgets this, it ends in a futile maze of verbiage." (p. 121)

Finally, theological language is similar to a language of personal relations. It therefore does not have the precision of the technical words of science, but it is more expressive. The denotations are more vague but the connotations are richer. The analysis of theological language as a personal language shows why religious knowledge must necessarily be revelatory: "All personal relations require revelation, because no knowledge of persons in general can lead to knowledge of the unique person." (p. 161) The word "knowledge" is thus freed from the narrow confines of science, because with it we can legitimately say, "I know him" which means a world apart from scientific knowledge. Hordern thus concludes that he has arrived at a response to the challenge of analytic philosophy when it asks whether one can properly speak of "knowledge of God" or whether one can consider theological statements to be properly cognitive. His response is: "Unless we artificially redefine the word 'knowledge' so that it means something drastically different from what it means in ordinary language, there is no good reason to deny the right of the Christian to speak of his knowledge of God." (p. 82)

3. Ferré, Poteat, Coburn

To round up the discussion of the type of analysis treated in this section, three piecemeal analysis of different aspects of theological language will be briefly summarized. These are all included in Dallas High's *New Essays of Religious Language*.[41]

---

[41] Dallas High, *New Essays in Religious Language* (New York: Oxford University Press, 1969).

Frederick Ferré in his article "Mapping the Logic of Models in Science and Theology" is concerned with showing that the notion of models which is quite relevant in science is likewise of importance in theology, because theology is not unconcerned with cognitive issues, and models function in such a way as to clarify the cognitive elements of statements. He explains: "If we continue to understand by 'model' that which provides epistemological vividness or immediacy to a theory by offering as an interpretation of the abstract or unfamiliar theory-structure something that both fits the logical form of the theory and is well known, we shall find models in abundance in theology." (p. 75) As examples he points to the parables used by Christ, the types of the Old Testament, and the anthropological concepts of Scripture. Christ himself is the one supremely reliable model for God.

Ferré believes that if the composite picture offered by the biblical model of reality is properly taken *as a model*, then the problem about the empirical claims of religious language will not be so problematic, because one would regard these empirical pseudo-claims as falling into that half of the model which should be read as logically irrelevant. In other words, when one has grasped the point of the model, all other elements are to be taken as secondary.

The importance of the use of models is expressed by Ferré thus:

> ... not only are the models of theology essential for the interpretation of theological discourse within the language using community ... but at least equally important... these models are necessary for the expressions of religious beliefs to the world at large. Apart from concepts intelligible to human minds, theology remains empty of meaning to friend and foe - as well as to the theologian himself. And it is in the *models* of theological theories, not in abstract theory itself that all intelligible theological ideas are rooted. (p. 83)

William Poteat, in his article "God and the Private I" tackles the task of pointing out the important peculiarities of the role the first person singular "I" in language in order thereby to suggest an analogy between the logical role in certain types of discourse of the concept "I" and of the concept "God". This in turn will illuminate the use of certain theological concepts. The greater part of the article is a critique on the main thesis of Gilbert Ryle's book, *The Concept of Mind*[42] which Poteat

---

[42] Gilbert Ryle, *The Concept of Mind* (London: Hutchinson University Library, 1949).

considers as an ambiguous assault upon the "priviledged access" theory of self-knowledge. He disagrees with Ryle's contention that "John Doe's ways of finding out about John Doe are the same as John Doe's ways of finding out about Richard Roe."[43] The falsity of the statement lies, according to Poteat, in the peculiar role in our language of the first person singular pronoun. He explains further:

> If we take seriously the logical peculiar role of "I" then we can explain how on the one hand it seems that "I" names is assimilable to reports of behaviour and yet how it is possible on the other hand for *me* to be aware of its naming something which is not assimilable in this way... However publicizable what is named by "I" may be, there is always *for me* something which cannot be put into public discourse. (p. 131)

In other words, when I use "I", I am talking both about what can be made public and what cannot, about that which can be put into language and that which cannot. "I" therefore is a logically extended concept. It is not only about *acts* but it is *for me* something more, namely, *the actor*. In so far as "I" can be put into language, it possesses transferability. It may be used by an indefinite number of people, but when used by any person, it means one and only one person. Thus it has only minimum transferability which means that "I" always functions reflexively. It names the namer.

Poteat goes on to say that accepting this logical amphibiousness of "I", one sees that the extent to which the "I" cannot be wholly assimilated into the structure of language is the extent to which it precedes essence and eludes system. "I" as a logically extended concept functions thus in theological discourse with such notions as freedom, fellowship, grace, reconciliation and other concepts alluding to experience which are on the borders of linguistically limited experiences subject to the restrictions of the world where articulation into words is necessary.

The analogy between the logically extended concept "I" and the concept "God" is finally pointed out by Poteat in the following:

> Just as we can meaningfully speak of the acts, behaviour, intentions, etc. of the self and even see that there is some kind of correlation between acts and intentions, using our ordinary subject-object form of discourse, and can do this without assuming

---

[43] *Ibid.*, 156.

> that the meaning of "I" is entirely exhausted in this discourse, we can speak of God's acts, behaviour and intentions, etc., in straight-forward subject-object discourse about events in the world without assuming that God is just the sum of events... In both cases an actor who is not assimilable in his acts is the presupposition of the form of discourse. (p. 136)

The last article in High's collection of essays is R. Coburn's "A Neglected Use of Theological Language". Coburn seems to have learned his lessons on the Wittgensteinian method well, since his article shows a painstaking care to clarify all concepts used and he insists throughout that he is merely treating *one* use of theological language.

The main point of the article is to show that a use of theological statements which has so far been uninvestigated is their functioning as answers to what Coburn calls "religious limiting questions". By "limiting questions", he means:

> ... a form of words which has the grammatical structure of a question, but which is such that a typical utterance of the form of words does not amount to asking a straight-forward question of either a theoretical or a practical sort. Rather such an utterance characteristically constitutes a piece of linguistic behaviour which simply expresses presence of some state or condition of the soul... (p. 218)

Examples of limiting questions are: "Why ought I to do what is right?"; "Why did this have to happen to me?"; "What is the ultimate significance of life?"; "Is there really a God?". The last two examples are typical *religious* limiting questions which are usually triggered off by moral or religious crises.

Theological discourse functions in different ways in answering such questions. For example the statement, "Jesus is the Christ" answers by drawing the questioner's attention to certain facts he has overlooked which prompted him to ask the question. Being made aware of these facts, he no longer feels inclined to raise the question, because his awareness has wrought a change in his spiritual condition. Some theological statements carry with them a pictorial aspect which tends to catalyze in those who hear them a certain perspective which removes the disquietude which impelled the asking of the question. Coburn concentrates on what he calls the normal functioning of theological language, namely, to give the religious limiting question a "logically complete answer". This means an answer, the acceptance of which is logically incompatible with continuing to ask the question. For example, a theological statement like "God made

the world to be as it is" answers the limiting question, "Why is the world
the way it is?" in such a way that, according to Coburn, further enquiry
is out of place. But this is the case only if "God" is used to designate
a person, because if the "making of the world" is something other than the
deliberate action of a person, there would be nothing peculiar in asking
for a deeper explanation. But if "God" is construed to be personal, and
accepting the other attributes appropriated to him, then it becomes odd
to enquire further why the world is as it is, once one has accepted the
view that "God made it to be as it is."

In thus elucidating one use of theological language, Coburn likewise
gives an explanation for the powerful tendency in Western theological tradition to speak of God in personal terms.

4. Appraisal

The various samplings of the last type of analysis of religious language treated in this section, are representative enough to show how such
an analysis can constructively illuminate the many facts of theological
talk. In general, the contributions treated show a remarkable freedom
from preconceived theories of how religious language should function.
Rather there has been a looking at how it is actually used. Although each
analyst dealt with a particular aspect and used different approaches and
methods, there is a significant convergence in the results of their analyses. They all, in one way or another, came to the insight that religious
language is personal, dynamic, self-involving, performative and makes use
of logically extended concepts understandable in a particular context.

Dallas High is particularly to be commended for his elucidation of the
different uses of belief statements which is a help for the theologian in
avoiding catagory mistakes which cause puzzles no less in theology than in
philosophy. William Hordern, in his analysis, made a thoughtful attempt
to specify the distinctive use of the theological language game in a particular religious tradition. J.A. Martin commends him especially for this:
"By underscoring the communal context, the paradigm employment in worship
and the biblical-Christological foundation of the theological language,
he (Hordern) has usefully distinguished it from religious language in
general, which is all too often characterized in deceptive generalities." [44]

---

[44] J.A. Martin, *The New Dialogue Between Philosophy and Theology* (New York: The Seabury Press, 1966), 160.

The piecemeal analyses offered by Poteat and Coburn are modest but worthwhile contributions, in as much as they make conscious some of the unreflected aspects of religious language. Anyone who has an understanding of the organizational importance of the individual elements of a structure to the intelligibility of the whole, will not fail to appreciate the value of such unpretentious analytical efforts. Finally, Ferré's preoccupation with theistic models emphasizes the importance of the semantic dimension of the problematic posed by theological language. No assessment of religious language is complete if it fails to consider this question of "what is, and what is the ontological status of the referent of religious language."[45] If theological or religious language is to perform the moral, aesthetical, ethical, psychological and other functions it should perform, it must ultimately and necessarily do so in a framework of conviction regarding what is real. Without the conviction of the reality of God and his attributes which religious and theological language assert, these cannot offer an ultimate sanction for moral and ethical presciptions. It is the same conviction which is responsible for the perception of the world as a distinctive pattern. And in the last analysis, the psychological aspect of religion would be empty and ineffective if the realities of God, of salvation, of sin, etc. do not constitute its basic moving convictions. Ferré's discussion of models bring the question of these realities to the fore, because these realities are what the models represent.

The insights of the different forms of analysis treated in this chapter, but most especially of the last group, are made use of in this work's own attempt to elucidate still other facets of creedal statements.

---

45 F. Ferré, *Basic Modern Philosophy of Religion* (Charles Scribner Sons, 1967), 170.

Chapter II

METHODOLOGICAL CONSIDERATIONS

Just as there are many ways of opening up an experimental frog depending on what one wants to find out, there are likewise as many ways of analysing statements depending upon the concern of the analyst. It is clear that the main method to be used in this thesis is analysis - linguistic analysis. But even this is not distinctive enough. The history of modern linguistic analysis from B. Russell to D.Z. Phillips shows that there are as many methods of linguistic analysis as there are linguistic analysts. It is therefore necessary to indicate the specific methods or approaches of linguistic analysis to be used in this work.

As a preview of the follwing sections and as a first global methodological proposition, it can here be generally stated that the overall approach, tone and orientation of this thesis will be Wittgensteinian, that is, according to Wittgenstein's philosphy of language of the later period. In the actual analysis of the creedal statements, J.L. Austin's methodological insights into the analysis of statements as linguistic acts will be made use of.

It is clear that the scope of this work does not demand a detailed and comprehensive exposition of the philosophies of either Wittgenstein or Austin. Only those aspects which will elucidate the method we adopt will be thoroughly discussed and illustrated.

I. *The Wittgensteinian Approach to Linguistic Analysis*

In order to establish Wittgenstein's main concern in analysing language, one must see this analysis in the context of his philosophy of language. Although the main interest here is in the linguistic analysis advocated by the later Wittgenstein, one has to go back to his early philosophy of language in the *Tractatus*. From there we shall trace the continuity of his philosophical concern but mark the rise of his new insights into the nature of language. This will prepare the ground for the discussion of the methodology of the later Wittgenstein which is the main method adopted by this thesis. Since this method will be used in the analysis of creedal statements which are a form of religious language, Wittgenstein's view of religious belief statements will be likewise discussed presupposing that in his treatment of the subject, however fragmentary, he is disclosing his linguistic insights and methods.

1. Linguistic Analysis in the *Tractatus*

Without here taking into account the ontological structure of the *Tractatus* which has been treated in Chapter I[1], we hasten to state Wittgenstein's theory of language in this early phase. His theory set itself the task of plotting the limits of language. In his own words:

> ... the aim of this book is to set a limit to thought or rather not to thought, but to the expression of thoughts; for in order to be able to set a limit to thought, we should have to find both sides of the limit thinkable (i.e. we should be able to think what cannot be thought). It will therefore be in language that the limit can be set and what lies on the other side of the limit will simply be nonsense. (TLP, p. 3, Preface)

He set about doing this task by what may be called the "picture theory" of meaning and the "truth function theory". The basic idea of the first theory lies in the interpretation of the meaning of a proposition as that to which it refers in a picturing way. Language is the totality of propositions (TLP, 4.001) and propositions are models of reality (4.01). Reality or the world is the totality of facts (TLP, 1.1) which are mirrored in language. Analysis of ordinary propositions concerned with finding out their meaning, consists in breaking them down to their smallest units, the elementary propositions. An elementary proposition is a "concatenation of names," (TLP, 4.22) and a name means an object: "The object is its meaning." (TLP, 3.203) Whenever a proposition pictures a fact, the names which constitute it picture objects. The ultimate constituents of language are elementary propositions and names. Analysis means determining the meaningfulness of propositions by breaking them down into these components and establishing the meaningfulness of these by showing their correspondence to reality, that is, by determining the facts and objects they denote.

The "truth function theory" is closely related to the "picture theory". It is concerned with showing how propositions are related to one another. The precise question is: "What is the exact relationship between an ordi-

---

1 See Chapter I, p. 8.

nary proposition and an elementary proposition?" Wittgenstein's answer is that all non-elementary propositions are truth functional compounds of elementary propositions: "A proposition is a truth-function of elementary propositions." (TLP, 5) This means that the truth value of a compound proposition is completely determined by the truth values of its components. Once the truth value of its components are given, the truth value of compound propositions can be calculated. (TLP, 4.26) All propositions are related to elementary propositions truth-functionally. Elementary propositions, on their side, can be true or false depending on whether they match up with the world or not. The truth or falsity of propositions is thus determined not by other propositions but by the world, more precisely, by the correspondence of their constituent elementary propositions with the atomic facts of the world. Meaningfulness of propositions is likewise established by breaking down the propositions into their elementary components which are then judged meaningful by their agreement with the facts of the world. Thus the concern of analysis for meaning coincides with its concern with truth or falsity. And both are established by the breaking down of complex propositions into the elementary propositions and determining the correspondence of these latter to the facts of the world.

The above explanation suffices as a basis of understanding the shift in the concern of linguistic analysis advocated by the later Wittgenstein who gained new insights into the phenomenon of language. Wittgenstein's earlier theory of language was aprioristic and it was beset by many difficulties, the most formidable of which was the impossibility of getting hold of even just one elementary proposition, which was the fundamental factor in the "picture theory" of language as has been shown. The task of the later Wittgenstein remained the same, namely to understand language, but there came a fundamental shift in methods - from the essentialistic approach to the more empirical, situational one.[2] It is not necessary to discuss the continuity or the novelty of the thoughts involved in the second phase of Wittgenstein's philosophical career. The task here is merely to show the insights responsible for the methodological shift and how this changes the whole approach and ways of doing linguistic analysis. The following sections will therefore explain the new insights about language and illustrate the methods and techniques which affect the methods used in this study.

---

2 Cf. K.T. Fann, *Wittgenstein's Conception of Philosophy* (Los Angeles: University of California Press, 1969), 42.

2. Wittgenstein's Later Views On Linguistic Analysis

An important change in Wittgenstein's view of language is stated by the *Philosophical Investigations* thus: "For a large class of cases - though not for all - in which we employ the word 'meaning' it can be defined thus: the meaning of a word is its use in the language." (PI, 43). Meaning is thus no longer taken as a one to one correspondence of the word with reality. Again there is no need to go into the subtleties involved in this programmatic statement. But its main implications need to be explained. This insight has negative as well as positive aspects. Its negative aspects are those which express criticism of the "picture theory" of meaning. These can be summarized in five points.[3]

1. The *Tractatus* had used the word "meaning" to signify the thing that corresponds to the word. But this is to confuse the meaning of a name with the bearer of the name. Thus when Mr. Jones dies, the bearer of the name "Mr. Jones" dies - but not the meaning of "Mr. Jones", or else it would make no sense to say, "Mr. Jones is dead." (PI, 40)

2. The *Tractatus* had assumed an absolute one to one correspondence between the simples of language and those of reality. But it makes no sense to speak of breaking reality down into absolute simples, because the word "composite" and "simple" are used in "enormous number of different and differently related ways." (PI, 47)

3. The analysis as conceived by the *Tractatus* "as the breaking down of complex propositions into more elementary propositions" does not necessarily make the meaning of a proposition clearer: "Suppose that, instead of saying, 'Bring me the broom' you say, 'Bring me the broomstick and the brush which is fitted on to it' - is he going to understand the further analysed sentence better? This sentence, one might say, achieves the same as the ordinary one, but in a more roundabout way." (PI, 60)

4. The "picture theory" had assumed that a proposition is meaningless, if it does not have an absolutely determinated or exact sense, but "if I tell someone 'stand roughly here' - may not this explanation work perfectly? But isn't it an inexact explanation? Yes, why shouldn't we call it 'inexact'? Only let us understand what 'inexact' means. For it does not mean 'unusable'." (PI, 88)

---

[3] Cf. D. Hudson, *Ludwig Wittgenstein* (London: Lutterworth Press, 1968), 42 f.

5. The *Tractatus* had claimed that a meaning is given to the proposition by a mental act distinct from uttering the sign - "by thinking the sense of the proposition." (TLP, 3.11) The *Philosophical Investigations* show by numerous examples that it is not possible to use conventional words and mean by them arbitrary meanings: "When I do it, I blink with effort as I try to parade the right meanings befor my mind in saying the words... When I say the sentence with this exchange of meanings I feel that its sense disintegrates." (PI, p. 176)

These negative aspects of Wittgenstein's insights already hint at the new positive insights into language and the consequent effects on the method of its analysis. Some key concepts of Wittgenstein's view of language in this later phase which are made use of by this study are "language games", "forms of life", "surface and depth grammar", "family resemblances". Since these concepts are woven into one another, they will not be discussed in isolation but in relation to each other.

In trying to understand what the concept *language game* is all about, Wittgenstein's fundamental insight must be recalled, namely, that in most cases, the meaning of a word is its use in the language. By "use" Wittgenstein means the actual conventional use in the language and not some arbitrary use that can be made of it by a speaker. The actual use of a word in a language follws certain rules - the grammar rules. Wittgenstein makes a distinction between *surface* and *depth grammar*. (PI, 664) The first is constituted by the rules of correct sentence construction. Depth grammar shows modal differences and semantic nuances. Perhaps an example can best show the difference. "To sew a dress" and "to knit a dress" have similar surface grammar. But the depth grammar shows a great difference. In the first example, a material, i.e. cloth, is necessary. In the second, the material is created by the action of knitting. In a greater degree, this difference is exemplified by the statements: "Number series are infinite" and "God is infinite" which need further explanation. Depth grammar illuminates the way certain phrases or words are used in different context. The use of words and sentences in the context of different situations and activities, linguistic and non-linguistic, is what is described by Wittgenstein's useful but sometimes misunderstood term "language game".[4] In his own words: "I shall call the whole, consisting of language and the actions into which it is woven, the 'language game'". (PI, 7) These speech activities use words and sentences in countless ways and this multiplicity is not something fixed but the new types come into existence and others become obsolete. (PI, 23) As examples of language games, Wittgenstein lists the following:

> Giving orders and obeying them -
> Describing the appearance of an object, or giving its mearurements -
> Constructing an object from a desciption (a drawing).
> Reporting an event -
> Speculating about an event -
> Forming and testing a hypothesis -
> Presenting the results of an experiment in tables and diagrams -
> Making up a story and reading it -
> Play-acting -
> Singing catches -
> Guessing riddles -
> Making a joke; telling it -
> Solving a problem in practical arithmetic -
> Translating from one language into another -
> Asking, thanking, cursing, greeting, praying. (PI, 23)

These language games are related to each other not by one common essential characteristic, but by "family resemblances." (PI, 67) There is not one single distinctive note which is or must be present in all these activities. There is a great deal of overlapping of characteristics, but there is no definite line of demarcation that can be drawn between them.

The term "language game" is meant to put into prominence the fact that the speaking of language is a part of an activity or of a *form of life*. (PI, 23) A "form of life" is constituted by the human activities and behaviours which are involved in a specific linguistic activity that takes place. In a true Wittgensteinian manner, this can be made clear by means of examples. One who says, "It is three o'clock, you will be late for class", and says it meaningfully, shows that he can read the clock or can tell time in some other way, that he knows how to measure duration, that he

---

[4] The term "language game" gives the impression that there is something trivial and inconsequential about it. But nothing is farther from Wittgenstein's mind than this aspect of "game" when he coined the term. He used it to bring into prominence the fact that the speaking of language is a part of an activity - of a form of life. A word in language can therefore have many varied uses depending upon the activity or activities which accompany it. This is exemplified by the word "game" which is used for an almost infinite number of activities which have overlapping characteristics but do not have one essential character which justifies their being called "games."

experiences the befor and after of time, etc. Wittgenstein claims that even if a lion could utter words, we would not really understand him, (PI, 223) if this general behaviour is in every other respect, exept for the ability to utter words, like that of any ordinary lion. We would not understand him, since he does not share the relevant forms of life with us. The "talking" of animals in cartoons, fables and fairy tales are meaningful only, because the animals are depicted as behaving like human beings.

In the light of these insights, analysis of language can no longer consist in resolving something into its elements or constituent parts. Analysis will henceforth take on the sense of examining critically for the sake of understanding the nature or organization of that which is to be analysed or to study the different factors involved in it. Philosophical linguistic analysis which is concerned with understanding and meaning will thus study the factors that go into the meaningfulness of propositions - namely the uses of words and sentences, the different contexts in which they occur, the activities and the forms of behaviour that accompany them as well as the presuppositions that underlie the different language games. This way of investigation might aptly be termed "linguistic phenomonology" but without the essentialistic nuance of Husserl's phenomonology.[5] The concern of this philosophical activity is the clarification of language. It will be a "battle against the bewitchment of our intelligence by means of language". (PI, 109) It is therefore therapeutic although not necessarily exclusively so[6], because it can be used not only to dissolve philosophical problems, but also for some constructive projects such as the understanding of different types of discourse, of which this study is an example.

In this latter type of linguistic analysis, Wittgenstein uses several techniques and methods amply illustrated in his book, *The Philosophical Investigations*. We shall explain and illustrate only that which we have taken over in our own analysis. In this latter method, Wittgenstein, in studying the meaning of words or phrases, does not resort to definitions,

---

5 For a brief explanation of the phenomenology of Husserl' see "Phänomenologie" in *Das Fischer Lexikon: Philosophie*, 1967ed., Vol. I, 243.

6 Richard Bell implicitly shares this view that the Wittgensteinian method is not exclusively therapeutic when he uses the method in declineating the functions of what he calls "descriptive theology". For details, see R. Bell, "Wittgenstein and Descriptive Theology", *Religious Studies*, II (October, 1969), 1-18.

theories, or systems. He rather uses what he calls "perspicuous representation." (PI, 122) This consists in tacing the contours of the word or phrase by means of examples of activities or objects that are covered by the concept being analysed. He shows the similarities or differences between these activities or objects. For this he uses what he calls "intermediate cases" (PI, 122) which lie in a continuum between two types of activities or objects designated by the same word. After one has gotten the "feel" of the word or phrase by analysing all its different nuances, it is then compared or contrasted with words that designates other activities or objects no longer belonging to the word or phrase analysed but which still have similar characteristics as these activities or objects. There is no better way of illustrating this Wittgensteinian method than by quoting in full Wittgenstein's own delineation of the word "game":

> Consider for example the proceedings that we call "games". I mean board-games, card-games, ball games, Olympic games, and so on. What is common to them all? Don't say: "There must be something common, or they would not be called 'games'" - but *look and see* whether there is anything common to all. - For if you look at them you will not see something that is common to all, but similarities, relationships, and a whole series of them at that. To repeat: don't think, but look! Look for example at board-games, with their multifarious relationships. Now pass to card-games; here you find many correspondences with the first group, but many common features drop out and others appear. When we pass next to ball games, much that is common is retained, but much is lost. - Are they all 'amusing'? Compare chess with noughts and crosses. Or is there always winning and losing, or competition between players? Think of patience. In ball games there is winning and losing; but when a child throws his ball at the wall and catches it again, this feature has disappeared. Look at the parts played by skill in chess and skill in tennis. Think now of games like ring-a-ring-a-roses; here is the element of amusement, but how many other characteristic features have disappeared! And we can go through the many many other groups of games in the same way; we can see how similarities crop up and disappear.
> And the result of this examination is: we see a complicated network of similarities overlapping and criss-crossing; sometimes overall similarities, sometimes of detail. (PI, 66)

In order to sharpen the focus, Wittgenstein's analysis can be continued in the following manner: One could gather examples that lie in the vicinity of the word "game" but are no longer designated by it. One could bring in the word "dance" and show that the activity of dancing shares the recreational aspect and the physical movement aspect of "game". One could show that "dance" shares the aspect of timing physical actions with music with some types of games like parlor games but not with other games like football, baseball, etc. One can even show that some kind of dances could be "games", for example the "potato dance", the "candle dance",etc., but that there are types of dances that are not considered games like the classical ballet or the formal dinner dance, and so on.

This kind of analysis escapes the arbitrary limitations of a definition, a theory, or a system, thus doing justice to the concept one is analysing and avoiding pseudo-problems to which arbitrary limitations of the concept can give rise.

Although there will be a section in this chapter which states in what way this study makes use of Wittgensteinian insights and methods, it can already be said here that this method of perspicuous representation by means of intermediate cases will be the main technique used in describing the language game of confessing one's belief.

There still remains to be discussed some thoughts of Wittgensteinian on belief statements.

II. *Wittgensteinian Approach to Religious Belief*

Wittgenstein had some fragmentary reflections on religious belief which are relevant in one way or the other to this study of an aspect of religious belief, namely its expression in creedal statements.

1. In the *Tractatus*

In the *Tractatus*, Wittgenstein allowed no articulation of religious belief. The reasoning goes like this: "To understand a proposition is to know what is the case, if it is true." (TLP, 4.023) In another place it is stated: "... in order to be able to say '"p" is true (or false)', I must have determined in what circumstances I call "p" true and in so doing I determine the sense (Sinn) of the proposition!" (TLP, 4.063) In order to verify it, "we must compare it with reality," (TLP, 2.223) By reality, Wittgenstein meant the world. But God, in as much as he is deemed transcendent is beyond the world. But "the world is all that is the case" (TLP, 1) Therefore propositions about God who transcends the world cannot be pictures of what is the case. They must therefore be beyond what can meaningfully be said.

2. In the *Lectures and Conversations* and *Philosophical Investigations*

With the overcoming of the "picture theory", the approach to religious language was bound to change. Wittgenstein's later views on the matter is treated in the posthumously published *Lectures and Conversations on Aesthetics, Psychology and Religious Belief*, but his approach to religious language can likewise be deduced from the insights of the *Philosophical Investigations*.

In the *Lectures and Conversations*, there is a marked devaluing of empirical evidence as a necessary condition of religious belief. Religious belief is not a "matter of reasonability" (LC, p. 57) in the scientific or strictly logical sense. Its evidences are not those invoked by science or history. For the later Wittgenstein, religious belief has something to do with regulating one's whole life, (LC, p. 54) not with describing it. It is "using a picture", (LC, p. 59) and having it constantly in the foreground of one's thinking, thus regulating one's life. He emphasizes the importance of the training involved in the "techniques" of religious belief, i.e. in using a picture. Children born in a Christian milieu learn the techniques of using the specific Christian use of the picture. In a sort of second reflection, theology takes the picture as used by believers and defines the techniques of using it.

Wittgenstein relates theology to religious belief as grammar is to language. In PI, 373, he writes: "Essence is expressed by grammar. Grammar tells what kind of object anything is. (Theology as grammar)" The parenthetical remark in this context shows a relationship between theology and language in general. Understanding any form of expression entails not only words but also the actions into which these words are woven. The patterns which are formed by the total activity of speaking, the whole environmental language situation is its grammar[7]. Grammar, that is, our patterns of linguistic behaviour, contains in it, so to speak, the world, all facts. It tells "what kind of object anything is." What men do and say form the grammar of their language. In a similar way, theology expresses a particular form of life. It expresses a behavioural pattern whereby the concept "God" informs, constitutes and directs the activity of speaking in this form of life.[8] Just as grammar shows what it would or would not make sense

---

7 *Ibid.*, 17.
8 *Ibid.*, 18

to say in a language, so theology shows what it does or does not make sense to say in a religion. In other words, theology reveals the structure of religious belief.[9] But just as grammar depends on certain presuppositions, namely the conditions of human life, so does theology depend upon some presuppositions of a particular faith community. And here is where the discussion of this section finds its relevance in a work that concerns itself with creedal statements. It is necessary in the elucidation of the presuppositional role of creedal statements in theology and religious language in general. This will be the burden of a separate chapter.

III. *J.L. Austin and the Analysis of Statements*

In order to avoid interminable but for this work unnecessary discussion about Austin's philosophy, it is once again important to pinpoint the precise concern of this section with regard to this philosophy. First of all, there is no intention of relating Austin to Wittgenstein, though such an undertaking is possible, even fruitful and interesting.[10] Furthermore, a discussion of the whole of Austin's philosophy of language still goes far beyond the scope of this thesis. Discussions will be limited to the "performative theory" and the "force theory" but placing them in the context of the general framework of Austin's philosophy.

Two assumptions underlie Austin's method of linguistic analysis; first that language reveals how the world is categorized, and second, "that if a system of thought has been functioning successfully for a long time, the distinctions underlying its classifications of its objects will be well founded."[11] Given these two assumptions, it was natural for Austin to concentrate on ordinary language and thus he conceived his task as a philosopher "the careful elucidation of the forms and concepts of ordinary language (as opposed to the language of philosophers, not to that poets, scientists or preachers)".[12] The above presuppositions and philosophical

---

9 D. Hudson, *Op. Cit.*, 17.

10 For a comparative discussion of Austin and Wittgenstein, see: D. Pears, "Wittgenstein and Austin" in B. Williams and A. Montefiori (eds.) *British Analytical Philosophy* (London: Routledge and Kegan Paul, 1966), 17-40; and Jerry Gill, "The Tacit Structure of Religious Knowing" in *International Philosophical Quarterly*, IX (December, 1969), 533-559.

11 D. Pears, *Ibid.*, 20.

12 J.O. Urmson, "John Langshaw Austin" in *Encyclopedia of Philosophy*. 1st. ed., I, 211.

concern gave rise to a rigorous technique of analysis which is not necessary to describe here. The important thing to note is that this technique lent itself to a set of independent enquiries, two of which are significant here, namely, those which led to the "performative theory" and to the "force theory."

1. The Performative Theory

The "performative theory" was first hinted at in Austin's article "Other Minds"[13] published in 1946. The kernel of this theory is the performative-constative contrast which is explained in *How To Do Things With Words*.[14] Austin observed that a great number of utterances, even those in the indicative mood, were such, that in some contexts, it would be impossible to characterize them as either true or false. For example:"I name this ship 'Queen Elizabeth'". This is a part of christening a ship and not a statement about the christening of a ship. Another example is: "I promise to meet you tomorrow." Again this is *making* a promise and not a report of a promise or a statement about what will happen. These utterances or statements Austin called "performative" to indicate that they are the performance of some act and not the report of its performance. In contrast to these utterances, Austin coined the term "constative" to designate all utterances that are *prima facie* predicated either true or false. Mats Furberg succinctly shows the difference betwee the two thus: "The facts reported by the constative can exist whether or not the constative is issued; but performatives constitute the fact they seem to report."[15] There are two kinds of performatives, the primary (implicit) performative which performs without using the explicit verb characterizing the performance, and the explicit performative which uses such a verb. Examples to show the difference between the two are:

1. *implicit, primary performative*:
    "I will come tomorrow."
    "I am sorry."

---

13 J.L. Austin, "Other Minds" is also included in the volume: J.L. Austin, *Philosophical Papers* ed. by J.O. Urmson and G.J. Warnock (London: Oxford University Press, 1970), 111-133.

14 J.L. Austin, *How To Do Things With Words* (London: Oxford University Press 1962).

15 Mats Furberg, *Saying and Meaning* (Oxford: Basil Blackwell, 1971), 200.

2. *explicit performative*
   "I *promise* to come tomorrow."
   "I *apologize*."

For a performative to constitute the fact it seems to report, in Austinian terms, "for a performative to be felicitous", it must fulfill certain conditions. In *How To Do Things With Words*, these are summarized as follows:

> (A.1) There must exist an accepted conventional procedure having a certain conventional effect, that procedure to include the uttering of certain words by certain persons in certain circumstances, and further,
> (A.2) the particular persons and circumstances in a given case must be appropriate for the invocation of the particular procedure invoked.
> (B.1) The procedure must be executed by all participants both correctly and
> (B.2) completely.
> (C.1) Where, as often, the procedure is designed for use by persons having certain thoughts or feelings, or for the inauguration of certain consequential conduct on the part of any participant, then a person participating in and so invoking the procedure must in fact have those thoughts or feelings, and the participants must intend so to conduct themselves, and further
> (C.2) must actually so conduct themselves subsequently. (HDTW, 14 f.)

A performative violating one or more of the felicity conditions (A.1-B.2) is considered a *misfire*. That means that one has not managed to perform the intended act. If a performative satifies these first conditions but not one or both of the C-conditions, the act is nevertheless brought off. A promise done in bad faith is still a promise. It is not considered a misfire but an *abuse*. For the purpose of this study, the above simplified treatment of the "performative theory" is sufficient.[16]

2. The Force Theory

The "force theory" is mainly explained in the latter part of *How To Do Things With Words*. Again it is unnecessary here to trace the development of the theory nor to speculate whether it supplants the "performative theory" or not. Austin's discovery of the performative is a valuable insight into the workings of language and it should not totally disappear

---

16 For a more detailed treatment of this theory, see *Ibid.*, Chapter V, 192-252.

into the background. It will in fact be used in this study to point out distinctions which it can bring out more effectively than the "force theory".

The main impulse of the "force theory" is the insight that "stating" taken in its concrete speech situation is likewise "performing", i.e. performing a speech act. Austin relates the two theories thus: "The doctrine of performative/constative distinction stands to the doctrine of locutionary/illocutionary acts (force theory) in the total speech act as the special theory to the general theory." (HDTW, 147) The "force theory" distinguishes three speech acts, the *locutionary* act, the *illocutionary* act, and the *perlocutionary* act, and identifies five illocutionary forces, namely, the *verdictives*, the *exercitives*, the *commissives*, the *behabitives*, and the *expositives*. The locutionary act is the "utterance of certain words in a certain construction and the utterance of them with a certain 'meaning' in the favourite philosophical sense of the word, i.e. with a certain sense and with a certain reference." (HDTW, 94)

To perform a locutionary act in general is *eo ipso* to perform an illocutionary act, which is so to say a specification of the use one makes of the locution, namely, asking or answering a question, giving some information or an assurance, announcing a verdict or an intention, pronouncing a sentence, making an appointment or an appeal or a criticism, etc. The *illocutionary* act is therefore the performance of an act *in saying* something as opposed to the performance of an act *of saying* something.

Furthermore, there are certain occasions when to perform a locutionary act and therein an illocutionary act may also be to perform an act of another kind, that is, saying something which normally produces certain effects upon the feelings, thoughts or actions of the audience, the speaker or other persons, and it may be done with the intention of producing them. The resultant act Austin terms *perlocutionary act*. The examples he gives to show the distinctions between these three acts are the following:

(E.1) Act (A) or *Locution*
He said to me "Shoot her" meaning by 'shoot' shoot and referring by 'her', her.
Act (B) or *Illocution*
He urged (or advised, ordered) me to shoot her.
Act (C.a) -*Perlocution*
He persuaded me to shoot her.
Act (C.b) He got me to (made me) shoot her.

(E.2) Act (A) or *Locution*
He said to me, "You can't do that."
Act (B) or *Illocution*
He protested against my doing it.
Act (C.a) -*Perlocution*
He pulled me up, checked me.
Act (C.b) He stopped me, he brought me to my senses.
(HDTW, 101 f.)

With regard to the *illocutionary forces*, it must be said at the outset that the grouping of these forces under their respective headings is not an absolute distinction. There are no clear-cut boundaries distinguishing one group from the other. Under certain aspects, certain verbs can belong to one or the other group. Furthermore, each group entails some other as will be shown in the treatment of the various groups.

The group of verbs that fall under the classification, *verdictives*, is typified by the giving of decisions by a jury, arbitrator or umpire. These verbs perform a judicial rather than legislative or executive acts. Examples are "I acquit, convict, interpret as, reckon, rule, estimate, date, place, make it, grade, assess, rank, value, analyse, characterize." These may be put under the other headings from some other aspects. They are verdictives in their aspect of "giving a finding as to something, fact or value which is for different reasons hard to be certain about." (HDTW, 150) They are decisions of "what is" rather than "what should be" which is the case of the exercitive. Thus in a basketball game a referee announces that a certain player has committed a foul. Because of the speed of the players and for some other reasons, this cannot be easily ascertained by the watchers, so the referee makes an assessment of the situation. This example likewise shows the involvement of verdictives with some other group of verbs, in this case, the exercitives. With the referee's ruling that a foul has been committed comes an exercitive decision that the player who has committed the maximum number of fouls must go to the bench and that the player against whom the foul is committed gains one or two free baskets. This brings the discussion to the exercitives.

An *exercitive* is a linguistic act which gives a decision against or in favour of a certain course of action. (HDTW, 215) Unlike the verdictive, it is a decision that something *should be* so and not a decision that *it is so*, as shown in the above example. Other examples are "I appoint, degrade, dismiss, name, order, sentence, fine, choose, vote for, bequeath, pardon, resign, advise, plead, pray, urge, proclaim, announce, annul, reprieve, veto." All these verbs have an advocative aspect; they decide that a state of affairs be created or should come to pass.

Commissives are typified by "promising or otherwise undertaking." (HDTW, 150) The point is that the speaker commits himself to a course of action. Examples are: "I promise, contract, undertake, bind myself, give my word, plan, guaratee, pledge myself, bet, consent, side with, favour, adopt." Again these verbs have differences among themselves. For example one promises to do something, but one bets that something will happen. There is an element of something unforseen present in betting which is not in promising. But both are commissive in their aspect of personally backing a course of action on the part of promising and a prediction on the part of betting.

Behabitives are a miscellaneous group and they are concerned with "attitudes and social behaviour." (HDTW, 151) They include the notion of reaction to other people's behaviour and of attitudes and expressions of attitudes to someone else's conduct. Examples are "I apologize, congratulate, command, condole, curse, challenge."

Finally, the *expositives* are used in acts of explanation "involving expounding of views, conducting arguments, and the clarifying of usages and reference." (HDTW, 160) Examples are "I affirm, remark, state, inform, ask, testify, report, accept, concede, interpret, distinguish, define, refer, call, understand, regard!" This group is the most fluid, because the examples can be easily grouped under the four preceding headings as well. Austin himself considers it troublesome and not in the least definitive. (HDTW, 151) It is just mentioned here for completion, but this study prefers to resort to the constative/performative distinction when it meets verbs of this type in its analysis.

As has been said before, these groupings flow into one another. Under certain aspects, certain verbs can belong to one or the other group. Furthermore, each group entails some other. For example, verdictives may commit one to some action that is necessary for the consistency with and in support of the verdict, as has been shown in the example of the basketball referee's decision. A positive evaluation of a cause can be an espousal of the cause. Exercitives can be very close to behabitives. For example, protesting and approving may be the taking up of an attitude as well as performing the act of challenging or protesting or praising. And so on.

It is to be noted that Austin makes the performative the paradigms of illocutionary forces and that the illocutionary forces, perhaps with the exception of the expositives, are subject to the same conditions for felicity cited in connection with performatives.[17]

Austin never made a coherent system out of the results of his painstaking and penetrating enquiries. Philosophers after him like Mats Furberg[18] and Donald Evans[19], recognizing the value of these studies, attempted to make some sort of systematization, reconciling seeming inconsistencies and making their own changes where inconsistencies are real. Here not even a systematization of Austin's analysis of statements is necessary. One can take the insights of independent enquiries, for example the two discussed above, and apply them to one's own investigations of a specific form of speech act. One needs only to adopt the main distinctions and disregard the borderline cases and the subtleties of the theories which tend to blur the distinctions.

IV. *The Adoption of Wittgensteinian and Austinian Methodology in this Thesis*

It remains now to show just precisely in what way this work will use the approaches discussed in the preceding sections. As has been said in the introduction to this chapter, the main orientation of the work as a whole is Wittgensteinian. In concrete, this means that in trying to understand the language game of confessing one's belief, the approach will not be essentialistic (i.e. finding out what the essence of a creed is) but situational and functional (i.e. studying the actual uses of the creed in different contexts and characterizing its forces as a speech act or acts). Here is where Wittgensteinian method of perspicuous representation by means of intermediate cases will come in.

This will entail first of all a survey of the contexts in the Christian form of life in which confessing one's belief actually occurs, and the different functions and purposes the creed is or has been called upon to serve.

---

17 See pp. 52-53 of this thesis.

18 Mats Furberg makes this systematization in his book, *Saying and Meaning*.

19 Donald Evans, *Logic of Self-Involvement* (London: SCM Press, 1963). In this book, Donald Evans uses the "force theory" to explore the performative aspect of the word "creation." The first part is a kind of systematization with some adaptations of Austin's enquiry into the performatives and into the illocutionary forces of speech acts.

From this a characterization of the inner forces of the speech act of confessing one's belief will be attempted. It is in this task that the Austinian analysis of statement will be used. More specifically, it will be assessed whether the creed is, in its primary intention, constative or performative. Furthermore, the different illocutionary forces of the creed will be determined from the consideration of its varied uses.

In a second reflection, the linguistic topography of the creedal statement will be mapped out by comparing/contrasting it to other forms of discourse in general and to the other religious uses of language in particular. This will be done through the introduction of intermediate cases.

The question of "meaning" of creedal statements will then be tackled according to the Wittgensteinian characterization of "meaning" as used in the language. This will show what uses of "meaning" apply to creedal statements as the specific form of speech act determined in the previous section. In other words, it will be discussed whether there is a sense in which creedal statements are said to be meaningful, and if so, in what sense. This will then lead to the significance of the act of confessing one's belief in the Christian context which will in turn throw light on the phenomenon of Christianity or the Christian belief as such.

As is true of most analytical studies especially in the line of Wittgenstein or Austin, this work will aim at clarification and not at synthesis or at the discovery of new properties of language. Although not primarily, it will also perhaps have a therapeutic aspect in the Wittgensteinian sense in that it hopes that by clarifying the language game of confessing one's belief as a speech act, it will dissolve certain irrelevant questions and pseudo-problems posed in connection with creedal statements.

PART TWO

THE LINGUISTIC ANALYSIS OF CREEDAL STATEMENTS

Chapter III

THE INNER DYNAMIC OF CREEDAL STATEMENTS

Creedal statements, which have been the topic of much philosophical discussions, are to be located in the religious activity of "confessing one's belief." It is by the investigation of the characteristics of this type of utterance that one will be made to feel the inner pulse of a creedal statement. In this chapter an attempt will be made to demonstrate these characteristics by:

1. observing the varied forms and uses of creedal formulae and creedal statements in the Christian way of life.

2. tracing the functions creeds have served in the Christian tradition.

3. gleaning from the diverse uses of creedal statements their varying forces as speech acts. Two supplementary topics, which do not essentially belong to the development of the topic will be discussed for the sake of completeness and as a help to understanding of the subject matter. These digressions will be on the non-Christian uses of creeds and on the creedal aspect of dogmatic statements.

I. *Creedal Statements in the Context of the Christian Life*

The activity of confessing one's belief takes a diversity of forms. Amid all differences in name, literary form, occasion of utterance and purpose, a most common family resemblance characterizes many of its forms as "a public avowal and formal statement more or less detailed, of the doctrinal content of religious belief, framed by an individual or by a group of individuals."[1] This is not a strict definition which excludes those which do not have one or the other characteristic it mentions. It just states the most common feature true to most of the forms of confession. This avowal may be addressed orally or in writing to a few persons, to a

---

[1] William Curtis, *A History of Creeds and Confessions of Faith* (Edinburgh: T&T Clark, 1911), 1.

congregation, to a church or to the public. It may be a brief spontaneous ejaculation of faith or a systematic treatise or doctrine.

The short, comprehensive formulae, which are dignified enough for use in public worship and are usually framed in the language of the first person, "I believe", "We believe", are known as *creeds*. The longer and more minutely systematic forms are technically termed *confessions*. Broken up and analysed into a series of questions and answers for didactic purposes, they become a *catechism*. Seen as a proclamation with an apologetic intention, of a distinctive doctrine, it is called a *manifesto, declaration* or *profession*. As a passport of admission to membership in a certain faith community, it is called a *symbol*. As a bond of union, it is a *consensus, covenant,* a *form* or *formula*. As a test of doctrine it is a *standard* or *rule of faith*. As a disavowal and condemnation of errors, it is a *syllabus*.[2]

In this work, only those forms of confessions of faith that are found in the Christian (Roman Catholic) context will be discussed. As has also been already mentioned in the introductory chapter, not only the utterance of official formulae, but likewise the private and spontaneous avowals of faith by believers in their daily life will be included in the treatment of the language game of "confessing one's belief." The following paragraphs will now locate the uses of the creeds in the Catholic way of life.

1. The Official Uses of the Creed

The most important of the traditional Christian creeds are the so-called *Apostles' Creed*, the Symbol of Nicea-Constantinople called the *Nicene Creed* for short, and the *Athanasian Creed*. These creeds are today used primarily in a liturgical context. The Nicene Creed is recited or sang at Holy Mass after the Gospel and before the Offertory. Its location in this part of the ceremony already says something of the kind of utterance it is meant to be. F. Amiot writes:

> The creed is well places at this point in the Mass as a profession of faith which had already been proclaimed in the chants and lessons. It takes on a character of pride in and glad adherence to the Christian message and thus forms an excellent introduction to the offering of the sacrifice.[3]

---

2 *Ibid.*, 3 f.

3 F. Amiot, *History of the Mass* (London: Burns and Oates, 1959), 61

The Athanasian Creed had been used before the liturgical reform as a hymn at Prime during the feast of the Holy Trinity. Another aspect of the creed is shown in the use of the Apostles' Creed in the baptismal rite. In the baptism of an adult, the catechumen usually receives instructions in the faith which is constituted usually by explanations of the articles of the creed. In the actual ceremony of Baptism, the adult recites the Apostles' Creed which receives a new characterization by this very act. This testimonial character is pointed out by the Dutch Catechism thus: "Was sich in einem inneren Prozess und in abgeschlossenen Lehrstunden abgespielt hat, wird nun öffentlich vor der Gemeinschaft und vor Gott gesagt."[4] In an interrogatory form, this profession of faith is renewed by the faithful during the Paschal Eve ceremonies. Sharing this renewal character is the singing of the Nicene Creed by the congregation at the end of the rites of Confirmation. Coming to the non-liturgical contexts, the Nicene Creed is sung at the end of every general papal audience.

There are several occasions where the profession of faith, oral or written, has been required within the Catholic Church.[5] These are:

1. in ecumenical or diocesan synods or councils by the delegates at the beginning of the council.
2. during the ceremony of receiving the red hat by those promoted to the cardinalate.
3. at the assumption of the office by bishops and abbots-elect.
4. at the beginning of one's academic career by rectors, professors of theology and philosophy in ecclesiastical institutions. (In some places, the professors and students still recite a profession of faith at the beginning of the scholastic year)
5. before reception of degrees in Catholic universities by Catholic candidates for higher degrees (usually for the Licentiate and Doctorate degrees).
6. at the assumption of office by superiors of clerical orders before they take over their office.

---

4 Die holländischen Bischöfe, *Glaubensverkündigung für Erwachsene*: Deutsche Ausgabe des holländischen Katechismus (Nymegen-Utrecht: Dekker & Van de Vegt, 1966), 274.

5 By order of Pius IV, the Profession of the Tridentine Faith was prepared in 1564 by a commission of Cardinals and was at once made obligatory on the whole *ecclesia docens* - Cf. W.A. Curtis, "Confessions" in *Encyclopedia of Religion and Ethics*, 1st ed., vol. III, 841. It must also be added that today, many of the examples cited have gone out of practice.

Until it was revoked recently, the oath against Modernism added to the profession of the creed was made by those who received the major orders, by confessors in receiving their faculties for hearing confessions, by the officials appointed to episcopal curias and to the sacred congregations in Rome, by theology and philosophy lecturers in religious houses of studies, and by superiors of religious congregations.

2. Private Uses of the Creed

The creeds have also non-official, private uses. Many theological and pastoral reflections on the faith make the creeds the basis for catechetical, theological and ascetical books. Priests frequently use one or the other article of the creed as subject matter for homilies and other forms of preaching. Lectures during spiritual retreats are often developed according to the structure of the creed. It forms part of the faithful's private devotion. The Apostles' Creed is often recited along with other prayers in saying the rosary. It is made the subject matter of meditations. It can even be the starting point of mystical insights as two examples will show.

St. Teresa of Avila writes in her classic work, *The Interior Castle*, that while reciting the Athanasian Creed, she got an insight into the mystery of the Trinity. In her own words: "Our Lord made me comprehend in what way it is that one God can be in three Persons. He made me see it so clearly that I remained as extremely surprised as I was comforted."[6] Martin Luther similarly records: "When a fellow monk, one day, repeated the words of the creed, 'I believe in the forgiveness of sins,' I saw the Scripture in an entirely new light and straight away I felt as if I were born anew."[7] One may quarrel about the nature of the insights involved in these examples. The point here is to show what role the creed plays in the religious life of those who utter them. In a less dramatic way but no less illustrative of the role of the creed in the Christian life is the writer's own recollection of how a beloved teacher's exhortation during the unstable years of adolescence to "take the first article of the creed and all its consequences seriously" had given her life its fundamental orientation.

---

6 Teresa of Avila quoted in W. James, *Varieties of Religious Experience: A Study of Human Nature* (New York: University Books, Inc., 1902), 411-412.

7 Martin Luther, quoted in *Ibid.*, 382.

The usual context of the private utterances of creedal statements in the daily life of believers is a limiting situation (Grenzsituation). People do not just utter creedal statements as a matter of course. Examples of such situations may be moments of perplexity in the face of life, incomprehensibility of painful experiences such as the death of a beloved one, sickness, loss of property, disaster or other incidents of misfortune. An official unjustly deprived of his office for political reasons may say: "I believe that God is just and he will see my cause through." It may also be a situation of excruciating doubt as described by St. Therese of Lisieux shortly before she died:

> He allowed my soul to be overrun by an impenetrable darkness, which made the thought of heaven, hitherto so welcome, a subject of nothing but conflict and torment... The darkness itself seems to borrow ... the gift of speech. I hear its mocking accents: "It's all a dream, this talk of a heavenly country, bathed in light... of a God who made it all, who is to be your possession in eternity. You really believe, do you, that the mist which hangs about you will clear away later on? But death will make nonsense of your hopes; it will only mean a night darker than ever, the night of mere non-existence."[8]

This wrings from her the cry of faith: "Suffering may reach the outermost limits, nevertheless, I am convinced that He will not abandon me!"[9]

A further light can be shed into the varied uses of the creed in Christian life by tracing the different functions it has performed in the course of its development. This necessitates a brief historical investigation into the origin of the Christian creeds and the role they played in Christian tradition.

II. *The Creeds in Christian Tradition*

In the treatment of the history of the creeds, the concern will not be to trace the development of the individual creeds in their contents or formulations, but rather in the uses to which they were put in the course of the centuries.

---

[8] Therese of Lisieux, *Autobiography*, tr. by Ronald Knox (New York: P.J. Kenedy and Sons, 1958), 255-156.

[9] Therese of Lisieux, *Geschichte einer Seele* (Trier: J. Zimmer Verlag, n. d.), 201. The passage is translated by the writer.

1. The Uses of the Creed in the Early Church

The very earliest creedal formulae consisted of short acclamations ascribing to Jesus of Nazareth one or more titles of honour - that is by confession that "He is the Christ," "He is Son of God," "He is Lord." (Mk. 8, 29; 1. Jo. 2, 22; Rom. 10, 9; 1 Cor. 8, 6; 1 Cor. 15, 32; 12, 3; Phil. 2, 11; Hebr. 13, 20; Jo. 2, 1; Acts 2, 36; Acts 22, 20) In the context of the Scriptures, these phrases form the kernel of the *Kerygma*. They are a proclamation of the good news of salvation. Neufeld writes: "The homologia 'Jesus is Lord' and the belief that 'God raised him from the dead' comprises the *rema tes pisteos* which is preached in the kerygma of the Church. Therefore the essentials of the Gospel which the Church proclaimed were closely related to the homologia to which the Christian community adhered."[10] These short phrases were used as acclamations in the worship services of the early Christian community and as such they exhibited another character. They were responses to the proclamation. They were an acknowledgement of, a testimony to, a confession of one's acceptance and adherence to it. They were likewise prayers of praise and adoration.

In the course of the growth of the Church, these short acclamations developed into formulae of faith with a Trinitarian structure which were used in baptism. The so-called *declaratory creeds* were used in the instruction of catechumens and the handing on of these creeds was termed *traditio symboli*. These creeds had principally an informative character and summarized the main tenets of the faith. They usually had three articles corresponding to the three Persons of the Trinity and generally enumerated the principal events in the life of Christ, his birth, suffering, death, resurrection and ascension into heaven from whence he shall come again. Later on the article on the Holy Spirit was expanded to include the ecclesial and eschatological articles. The creed was presented to the catechumen as an introduction to the unifying ideal of the Christian community inviting him to a decision of self-commitment.

In the baptismal rite itself, the *interrogatory creeds*, which have in kernel the same material content as the declaratory creeds, lose their informative role. In this *redditio symboli*, the assent to the creedal pro-

---

10 Vernon Neufeld, *The Earliest Christian Confession* (Leiden: E.J. Brill, 1963), 24.

positions become in a strict sense a profession of faith. This function is clearly discerned in the context of the rite described in the following:

> ... the convert first turned towards the west, the land of darkness, renounced Satan, his worship and his pomp; then he turned towards the rising sun and confessed his allegiance to Jesus Christ. This mental turning towards Jesus Christ as Lord meant turning away from all other lords. This first phase of the ceremony of baptism was called abjuration or renunciation... The before entering the baptismal pool, the candidate was asked these three questions: "Do you believe in God the Father Almighty?" The catechumen answered, "I believe." "Do you believe in our Lord Jesus Christ?" Answer: "I believe." And finally, "Do you believe in the Holy Spirit?" to which the answer was "I believe." Then three times the candidate was immersed or water was poured on his head. After he was re-dressed, his head was anoited with oil. He could then re-enter the Church building and join the group of believers.[11]

The function of the creed as a profession of faith reaches its fullest expression in the credo uttered by the martyrs in the arena. When arrested and brought before a court, Christians gave answers such as: "My true father is Christ and my mother is the faith by which I believe in Him." A free Roman citizen was wont to answer: "I am a slave of Christ." while a slave replied: "I am a free man of Christ." St. Afra answered her judges thus: "Salus mea Christus est, qui pendens in cruce, latroni confitenti bona paradisi pollicitus est."[12] In this context, the creedal utterance has an added function - that of being a testemony. This witness (*maturein*) character of the utterance is backed up by a radical self-commitment unto death. In such a limit situation, the creed likewise performs an inspirational function - as a reassurance and a motivation for the supreme act of sacrifice. It resembles the cry of the Old Guards of Napoleon who went into their death with "Vive l'Empereur!" In this sense, it is a battle cry.

2. The Rise of Synodal Creeds

Up to the fourth century, the creeds were primarily used in the contexts cited above, namely in worship, in baptismal rites, in catechetical instructions, in trials before the hostile crowds. With the development of the

---

11 Paul T. Fuhrmann, *An Introduction to the Great Creeds of the Church* (Philadelphia: The Westminister Press, 1969), 15.

12 Cf. Ruinart, T. *Acta Martyrum* (Vienna: Rieger, 1803), 79. Also, A. Loisy, *The Birth of the Christian Religion*, tr. L.P. Jacks (New York: The Macmillan Co., 1948), 332.

Church's self reflection and occasioned to a great extent by the exigencies of controversy, the creeds took on new functions. In the relations of the Christians to the non-Christian world, The creed was the open acknowledgement of the Christian way of life before pagan or Jewish opponents. The theological contoversies that rocked the Church provided another context for the utterance of the creed. These, in fact, gave rise to a new form of creed, the *synodal* or *conciliar creed* as distinguished from the baptismal creed. The difference between the two is put succinctly by C.H. Turner thus: "... the old creeds were creeds for catechumens, the new creed was a creed for bishops."[13] This might be an oversimplification, but the point is that a new function will be played by these new forms which was not served by the old baptismal creeds. These new creeds were not necessarily new formulae but were the same formulae as some baptismal creeds or adaptations of them supplemented with a string of anathemas directed against the specific heresy confronting the specific council. Two interrelated functions of the creed thus emerge: as a polemic against heretics and as a rule of faith to ascertain orthodoxy.

The Council of Nicea in the fourth century, wishing to define its belief against Arian heresy, reformulated an already existing baptismal creed of the Syro-Palestinian church to suit its purposes. The resulting change in nuance is noted by Kelly:

> The Nicene Creed was first and foremost a definition of orthodox faith for bishops. It was pronounced to smooth over a particular crisis in the Church. No one intended it, in the first instance at any rate, to supersede the existing baptismal confessions. Bristling with anti-Arian clauses and armed at the tail with polemical anathemas, it was hardly suited to be the solemn formula in which the catechumen would avow his adhesion to the Christian revelation.[14]

Not satisfied with merely demolishing the heretical position, the Nicene Creed made positive theological interpolations, the most important of which concerned the full divinity of the Son in a language which implied the doctrine of identity of substance (homoousios) between him and the Father. By so doing, the creed assumed a theological function similar but distinct from the reflections of private theologians. The distinguishing factor is its de-

---

13 C.H. Turner quoted in J.N.D. Kelly, *Early Christian Creeds* (London: Longmans, Green and Co., Ltd. 1960), 295.

14 Kelly, *Op. Cit.*, 255.

ciding aspect akin to the juridical pronouncement of a judge in court. It was meant to be a verdict against a particular stand in favor of another.

Another typically theological and dogmatic creed is the Athanasian Creed which had no liturgical foundation in its origin. It presupposed the Chalcedonian dogmatic decision and is the documentation of the results of the Trinitarian and Christological controversies of the early Church. According to Fuhrmann, it aimed mainly "to teach the vital tenets of Christianity to the clergy,"[15] at a time when the barbarian invasions threatened to wipe away Christian tradition along with the Hellenistic and Roman culture. There is thus the shift in function - from a profession of faith to teaching what one should profess. According to Schlink, it was not so much a liturgical confession as a doctrine about proper confession.[16] It is, however, only fair to put another opinion side by side with Schlink's which sees the synodal creeds as still having very much of a confessional character in spite of the new doctrinal nuance they have acquired. Ratzinger admits that this type of creed "nicht mehr im sakramentalen Zusammenhang des kirchlich vollzogenen Bekehrungsgeschehens, im Vollzug der Kehre des Seins und so im eigentlichem Ursprungsort des Glaubens verwurzelt ist, sondern aus dem Ringen der zum Konzil versammelten Bischöfe um die rechte Lehre stammt und damit deutlich zur Vorstufe der künftigen Form des Dogmas wird."[17] He insists however that the bishops did not yet formulate the doctrinal statements in the early councils but that "ihr Ringen um die rechte Lehre sich immer noch als Ringen um die Vollgestalt des kirchlichen Bekenntnisses abspielt."[18] Whatever the case may be, the point important here is the doctrinal character which the creed acquired.

The Nicene Creed, which was considered the expression of the faith according to the Scriptures, and recognized by the Church Fathers, became the touchstone of orthodoxy. The synodal creeds thus assumed a normative function over the faith of Christians in general and over the doctrines of teachers and leaders in the Church in particular. It was also this

---

15 Fuhrmann, *Op. Cit.*, 48

16 E. Schlink, *The Coming Christ and the Coming Church* (London and Edinburgh: Oliver Boyd Ltd., 1967).

17 Josef Ratzinger, *Einführung in das Christentum* (München: Kösel Verlag, 1968), 60.

18 *Loc. Cit.*

normative juridical function of the creed which was utilized by Constantine's successors to make the creeds the basis of political and ecclesiastical unity in the Empire. We have an example of this political use to which the creed was put in the following:

> Die erste kaiserliche Bekenntnisentscheidung ist mit dem Edikt der Kaiser Gratian, Valentian II und Theodosius I vom 27.2.380 gegeben. Dieses "Theodosianum"..., das Heiden und Häretiker entrechtete legt zugleich für die Reichskirche ein einheitliches und verbindliches Bekenntnis fest und bindet die "apostolica disciplina" und die "evangelica doctrina" an die Übereinstimmung mit der offiziellen Lehre der Patriarchate von Rom und Alexandrien. (RGG^3 I, 1003-1004)

The foregoing considerations bring to light still another facet of the creed, namely its conservative and traditional functions. In *Sacramentum Mundi*, we read: "Wenn es dem Lehramt zukommt, das Glaubensbekenntnis zu formulieren oder es in einem strittig gewordenen Punkt zu ergänzen, ist das Symbolum auch die Regel, auf die es sich beziehen muss - als Ausdruck der apostolischen Tradition."[19] And J. Pelikan writes:

> While it is true that the addition and the revision of the phrases in the creeds are an index to the evolution of the Church's teachings, it is also true that from the very beginning, the creeds were a conservative force as well, instructing the candidates and reminding the worshippers of what the Church had been believing, teaching, and confessing, which included some doctrinal themes that did not figure as prominently in Christian piety and instruction at one time as they had in another.[20]

3. The Creed in Later Church History

In the course of the centuries, especially in the Catholic Church, the theological-doctrinal development of the creed pushed its confessional character in the background. The conciliar decrees assumed a more magisterial character, although the conciliar Fathers continued to cite the Nicene Creed at the beginning of their decrees (DS, 1500) as their profession of faith and adopted the creedal structure by starting with "credimus" in their promulgations.

In the Middle Ages, the word "confitemur" was added to the "credimus." (DS, 790-792) This has a reason which is interesting for our concern to

---

19 "Symbola" in *Sacramentum Mundi*, 1st. ed., 1969, vol. IV, col. 794.

20 Jaros. Pelikan, *The Christian Tradition: A History of the Development of Doctrine*, Vol. I - *The Emergence of the Catholic Tradition (100-600)* (Chicago and London: The University of Chicago Press, 1971), 127.

detect the changing nuances in the confession of faith through the centuries. In the early formulations of creeds, the verb "credo" or "credimus" sufficed to show one's adherence to the tenets of the faith that followed the verb. This was the natural and ordinary expression of inner conviction. With the rise of the neo-Manichean heresies, particularly the Waldensians and Cathars[21] and the consequent intransigent fight against these heresies, there arose the danger of taking oaths of faith without really meaning them just to escape persecution. With the condemnation of these heresies and in the formulation of professions of faith against them came the use of the two verbs "credimus" and "confitemur" which is to be traced back to St. Paul's letter to the Romans, 10,10: "By *believing* from the heart you are made righteous, by *confessing* with your lips you are saved." This innovation was meant to re-emphasize the internal and external aspects that are supposed to be expressed by one and the same profession of faith. Later on, these verbs took on another grammatical form - from the first person to the third person. The First Vatican Council, for example, starts its decrees with "Sancta apostolica Romana Ecclesia credit et confitetur, unum esse Deum..." (DS, 3001) This reveals the growing trend towards that which is believed, away from the personal act of believing. The doctrinal aspect of the creed was gaining more and more attention. The personal act was, of course, not eliminated but was taken more and more for granted. Linguistically, this development is significant when one recalls Dallas High's analysis of belief statements emphasizing the distinction between the performative commissive force of the first person belief statement and the reporting or observing character of the third person belief statement.[22]

Another tendency which appeared in the course of history was to uniformity, which was a move away from the plurality of symbols allowed to the particular churches in the early centuries, especially in the East. This tendency towards uniformity appeared already in the West in the early Middle Ages, but it never came to an official banning of new formulations until the period of the Counterreformation. The Tridentine Creed (DS, 1862-1870) supplemented later on by the First Vatican Council (DS, 1869) and by the anti-modernist oath (DS, 3537-3550) became for sometime the remaining

---

21 Cf. Josef Lortz, *Geschichte der Kirche* (Münster: Aschendorffsche Verlagsbuchhandlung, 1959), 178-180.

22 See Chapter I of this thesis, p. 32.

official *professio fidei* of the Catholic Church aside from the three traditional creeds which she shares with the Protestant churches. The question of new formulations of faith or of a revision thereof was, for a time, out of discussion.[23]

The Second Vatican Council rejected a creedal schema prepared by a theological commission to serve as its official profession of faith.[24] The atmosphere created by this Council is however once again conducive to the discussion of the possibility of new, pluriform short formulations of the tenets of the faith, which would serve, not to replace the traditional creeds, but to supplement them and make their original function as a living expression of the faith of the community relevant and meaningful to the faithful of today, in the context of the radical changes in society and in the Church.[25]

So far we have gained an insight into creedal statements by tracing their uses and functions in the context of Christian life and tradition. To throw more light on the linguistic characteristics of these statements, we shall briefly descibe their functions in non-Christian contexts.

Digression A: Non-Christian Uses of Confessional Creeds

It is interesting to note that though confessional creeds are found in some non-Christian religions, they are not found in all. Zoroastrianism possesses such a creed which is found in a cultic part of the holy book *Avesta*:

> I drive the Daevas from hence
> I confess as a Mazda worshipper of the
> order of Zarathustra estranged from the
> Daevas devoted to the lore of the Lord,
> a praiser of the Bountiful Immortals;
> and to Ahura Mazda, the good and endowed
> with good possessions.
> I attribute all things good to the Holy One

---

23 Cf. K. Lehmann, "Bedarf das Glaubensbekenntnis einer Neufassung?" in *Veraltetes Glaubensbekenntnis?* (Regensburg: Verlag Friedrich Pustet, 1968), 139f.

24 Cf. Schema "Formula nova professionis fidei proposita a commissione theologica" (Vaticani, 1961) 12 pp. also G. Caprile, *II Concilio Vaticano*, II. I/2, 1961-1862 (Rome, 1966), 229.

25 Cf. Lehmann and Rahner "Kurzformel" in *Concilium*, III (1967), 200-207; and Otto Semmelroth, "Kurzformel des Glaubens und ihr Sitz im Leben" in *Geist und Leben*, vol. 44 (December, 1971), 440-452.

> the resplendent, to the glorious, whose are
> all things whatsoever which are good...[26]

Here we see explicitly positive and negative elements - a confession of loyalty to Ahura Mazda, the Lord and God, and a renunciation of the idols (Daevas) and their worshippers. The mention of Zarathustra points to the bearer of revelation. One use therefore of the creed in Christianity, namely the abjuration and a profession of loyalty in a liturgical context is also found in a non-Christian religion.

Another function of non-Christian creeds which has a parallel in Christianity is the use of the creed as an initiatory formula during the rites of incorporation into the religious community. An example of such an initiatory creed is the following Buddhist creedal formula:

> I believe in God
> I take refuge in Buddha
> I take refuge in the Dharma (doctrine)
> I take refuge in the Sangha (community)[27]

Still another use of a non-Christian creed which coincides with a function of the Christian creed is found in the context of worship. The famous creed of Mohammedanism, the Shahada, not only succinctly summarizes the main tenets of this religion and serves as an initiatory formula, but is likewise daily recited in the obligatory prayers of Mohammedans. The formula reads:

> I witness there is no God but Allah
> And I witness that Muhammad is the
> Apostle of Allah.[28]

Mohammedanism, like Christianity, is a religion which claims universality, and as soon as it launches its missionary activities, it is confronted with other religious communities and religious beliefs. In this confrontation, it is forced to determine its distinction from them in a process of self-reflection. These reflections are normally crystallized

---

26 Quoted in Max Müller (ed.), *The Sacred Books of the East*, vol. XXXI (Oxford: At the Clarendon Press, 1887), 247 f.

27 Quoted in William Christian, "Truth Claims in Religion" in Santoni, (ed.) *Religious Language and the Problem of Religious Knowledge* (Bloomington and London: Indiana University Press, 1968), 67.

28 Quoted in Wensinck, *The Muslim Creed* (Cambridge: University Press, 1932), 102.

and fixed into a creedal formula like the one cited above. There is however also a positive aspect of the creed in the missionary context. It is not just to set off one's belief against other beliefs. It is a positive witness to its convictions. It assumes the character of proclamation which directly aims at evoking a response from those who hear it.

From this brief consideration of non-Christian creeds, we discern the impulses that give rise to this type of utterance. One impulse is the experience of a revelatory event. The creed is an answer to revelation, in whatever manner this occurs. It is an assent which includes implicitly or explicitly a renunciation of that which goes contrary to the revelatory experience. Another impulse is the need of expressing one's solidarity with a faith community which one enters into not automatically by birth as in tribal religions, but after some sort of decision. The creeds also answer the need of fixing the position of the community in face of sects or of other beliefs. To do this, the community makes a summary of its own principal beliefs which are then used in prayer and worship as acts of adoration, praise and thanksgiving. In a missionary context, a creed serves as a direct proclamation aiming to convert.

Similar impulses as the ones cited above are also found in the confessional creeds of the Old Testament. The Hebrew creeds were primarily a reiteration of and a response to the self-revelation of Jahwe: "I am Jahwe, your God, who brought you out from the land of Egypt." (2 Moses 20, 2) To this, the people of Israel responded: "Yes, Jahwe is our God." This was not just at once and for all confession of faith, but as can be gathered from the context of Josua 24, 16 f., it was a liturgical formula that was uttered in the context of worship as a prayer of praise. This is likewise clear from the context of the dramatic episode at Mt. Carmel related in the Elias narrative (1 Kings 18). As the people of Israel saw the sign from heaven, they fell on their faces and cried out: "Jahwe is our God! Jahwe is our God!" (1 Kings 18, 39) The Psalms 80 and 50 have similarly enthroned this formula as praise of the wonderful works of Jahwe.

From these contexts, one sees that this creedal formula "Jahwe is our God" served to state who God is in answer to God's revelation of himself. He, who has done the wonderful works in behalf of Israel, He is Jahwe, the God and Lord of Israel. The formula was likewise Israel's pledge to the covenant which Jahwe freely entered into with his people. This gives the formula a forensic and binding character. On the part of Israel, it was a decision for Jahwe against the pagan idols. Again one notes the positive-negative elements of confessional creeds already seen in the non-Christian religions. Because of the communal aspect of this formula, it is able likewise to function as a common prayer in the public worship of the community.

This digression was meant to show the diversity of impulses and the corresponding diversity of uses that are involved in the confessional utterance. The ground is now prepared for the analysis of the linguistic forces of the creedal statement as a speech act.

III. *The Varying Forces of Creedal Statements*

The main focus is on Christian creedal statements. It is therefore helpful to summarize the functions of the Christian creeds as gleaned from the preceding sections:
1. First and simplest, the creeds were brief spontaneous utterances of conviction used as acclamations of gratitude, homage or adoration.
2. They were used as material for the instruction of converts and as a formula of admission in the rite of baptism.
3. In time, they were used in liturgical worship especially in the Eucharistic sacrifice.
4. They were uttered as a public testimony to the object of one's faith - public, not simply as made openly before the Church, but also before communities not sharing the faith.
5. They have been drawn up as vindication of the Christian belief and as such they were expositions of distinctive doctrines intended to remove misconception or to repudiate misrepresentations.
6. Similarly, they served to mark off true from false belief and therefore to settle theological controversies.
7. In a later function, creeds have served as a pledge of orthodoxy by office-bearers in the Church.

From these varied uses of creedal statements in the Christian context, we glean varying forces depending on their linguistic performance in different situations.

In this analysis, the Austinian distinctions between locutionary, illocutionary and perlocutionary forces will be used. It is important to note that this classification is artificial, because these forces can all be present in a single statement. They are inseparably bound to one another. The distinction is a distinction of aspects. Taken as such and not as absolute dichotomies, these distinctions can serve to clarify the various linguistic forces of creedal utterances.

1. Locutionary Forces of Creedal Statements

Creedal statements *are statements*. This tautology serves the purpose of emphasizing the aspect of a creedal utterance that has been underplayed in most linguistic analysis of religious language of the reductionistic type - namely that they do have cognitive, informative content.

Creedal statements used as material for instruction of any form (i.e. in the preparation of catechumens, in catechetical work, in missionary proclamation, in theological or philosophical discussions) exhibit locutionary forces. As an *Aussage*, the creed *expresses* the content of the Christian message. It *summarizes* and *states* the main tenets of the Christian faith. The speaker *describes*, makes *predications*, *asserts*, i.e. that Jesus is the Lord, that God is a loving Father, That Jesus was born of the Virgin Mary, etc. In a missionary context, it *proclaims*, therefore it *informs* people of what they do not yet know. As such it *makes truth claims*. It appeals to the cognitive powers of man, to his power of judging whether a certain predication or assertion is compatible with his experience of reality or not and to his power of discerning good grounds to adhere to them or not.

Although the locutionary aspect is not the *distinctive* force of creedal statements as speech acts (as it is in scientific statements or historical narratives for example), it is *basic* to the felicity of their illocutionary forces.

2. Illocutionary Forces of Creedal Statements

The survey of the functions of the creeds seems to point to the distinctive role of these forces in characterizing the linguistic act of confessing one's belief. In other words, creedal statements in their primary intention and use are meant to perform linguistic acts other than just stating. In a liturgical context, the creed is an expression of *praise*, of *adoration*, of *worship*. In the baptismal rite, the creed is a *pledge* or a *promise* to live up to the Christian way of life. It is an act of *adherence* to a community of faith. It is a *decision* which juridically binds the Christian to a distinctive form of life and which abolishes bonds other than that to which one has confessed himself. It is therefore an act of *renunciation* or *abjuration*. As a *symbolon*, it is a sign or *indicium* in the sense not only of a distinction between Christian and non-Christians, but also in the sense of a *tessera militum* a token or *deed of agreement* among Christians. In its use as a rule of faith, the creed is a *juridical pronouncement* of orthodoxy which is on one hand a *condemnation* of a doctrinal position and on the other a *commendation* of another position. The private spontaneous creedal utterances may be expressions of *trust*, *confidence*, *surrender*, *acceptance* of one's lot, or of *sympathy*, *encouragement*, and *consolation*.

3. Perlocutionary Forces of Creedal Statements

The question is whether the creedal statements possibly bring about an effect in others intended or unintended by the utterances.

In its communal aspect, the creed *establishes* a unity of faith and therefore is a *consensus* among men in a community of faith. It *creates* a sense of belonging together. Uttered in the context of martyrdom, it can *create edification* on one hand or violent *rage* on the other. It can likewise *inspire* faith in others, *console* them, *encourage* them. It can *convince* others and *urge* them to self-commitment. As has been shown in the case of some religious people, it can *trigger off* mystical insights.

These forces constitute the inner dynamic of creedal statements and it is important to point them out, because there is the danger of a one-sided treatment of these statements: on one hand of treating them exclusively as doctrinal assertions as is done by those who consider them as immutable photographs of eternal truths and on the other hand of denying their descriptive and assertive aspects as has been done by the reductionistic linguistic analysts. In either case, this type of utterance is misrepresented. Positively, these distinctions bring out the richness of nuance and the variety of performativeness of the language game of confessing one's belief.

To complete the discussion on the varying forces of creedal statements the question of dogmatic statements must still be treated. Dogmatic statements will be here taken to include the teachings of the ordinary Magisterium of the Church and the ex-cathedra pronouncement of the Pope and the binding pronouncements of the General Councils. The question will be confined to whether dogmatic statements are creedal statements and if so, what specific force do they exhibit in a distinctive way.

Digression B: Dogmatic Statements as Creedal Statements

Karl Rahner in his essay "What is a Dogmatic Statement?"[29] lists the creedal aspect as one of the distinctive characteristics of a dogmatic statement: "A dogmatic statement is a statement of faith." (p. 48) What precisely does this mean? Is a dogmatic statement a creedal statement in its material content? In its formal structure? In its force as a speech act? Is this claim or an imperative? Rahner's own elaboration seen in the light of the foregoing reflection on the varying forces of creedal statements will reveal the cognitive terrain of his assertion.

As regards material content, a philosopher analysing a dogmatic statement especially of the later part of Church History, will find it difficult to discern the substantial identity between these statements and the early creeds. This is something which a theologian presupposes or at least is able to trace. It needs theological presuppositions and theological methods to relate, for example, the dogma of the Assumption to the phrase of the creed, "born of the Virgin Mary." And what philosophical analysis can relate the dogmas on papal infallibility, on grace, on sin, etc. to the articles of the traditional creeds? It is the task of theology to set up theories on the development of dogma. It seems therefore futile for philosophy to try to establish a relationship of dogmatic statements and creeds from this aspect.

When one, however, looks at the dogmatic statement as a speech act, then one can establish such a relationship. Rahner himself presupposes the material continuity and elaborates the aspect of dogmatic statement as an *act of faith*. Faith, he maintains, is not only listening to the word of God; it is likewise already an understanding and an assent to it. The hearer already analyses, reflects on that which he hears and therefore a certain degree of theology is an intrinsic note of the hearing itself. (p. 48) Dogmatic statements are further developments, an unfolding of the basic subjective reflection which comes with the initial act of faith. (p. 48 f.) One is therefore to deduce from this that the act of dogmatic pronouncement by a council or by the Pope is an act of faith.

Furthermore, when one studies the forces of such dogmatic pronounce-

---

[29] K. Rahner, "What is a Dogmatic Statement?" in *Theological Investigations*, V, tr. by Karl and Boniface Kruger (Baltimore: Helicon Press, 1966), 48.

ments, one sees that they exhibit the illocutionary forces involved in the normative, juridical, conservative and traditional functions which they share with the synodal creeds even if the formal structures of both (namely, of dogmatic pronouncements and synodal creeds) no longer coincide perfectly. The dogmatic statement participates likewise in the doxological and witness character of the original creeds. Rahner writes:

> ... a dogmatic statement still participates in its own way in the expressed profession and praise of the message Christ has given us about himself and which leads us to him - in the expression of that message listened to and accepted. (p. 51)

Moreover, the dogmatic statement shares in the communitarian (ecclesiological) aspect of the creed. It is only in the context of a believing community that both the creed and the dogmatic statement gain significance, "for the act of faith is by hearing and remains dependent on the testimony of the message of Christ and this testimony takes place in the assembly of believers, originates from it and is destined for it!" (p. 52) The dogma of the Assumption, for example, is not just a statement about one woman in history; it is a commentary on a whole way of life lived through centuries; it has no meaning if it were just about any holy woman in history, not even if it were Mary, the mother of Jesus of Nazareth. Its significance is to be grasped only in the understanding of the role Mary has played in the Church, in its spirituality and in its tradition.

From the preceding considerations, one sees the grounds for *claiming* that dogmatic statements are creedal statements. As acts of faith, dogmatic statements exhibit the locutionary and perlocutionary forces exhibited by synodal creeds. The locutionary force has been overemphasized in the past. there has been an almost exclusive focus on that moment of dogmatic statements as propositions guaranteed by the authority of God, as an "expression of the unchanging truth." Rahner's attempt to relate it to the original assent of faith is a move to release its less explored illocutionary forces. Rahner's assertion "A dogmatic statement is a statement of faith" seems rather more of an imperative than an indicative statement.

Chapter IV

THE LINGUISTIC TOPOGRAPHY OF CREEDAL STATEMENTS

The preceding chapter attempted to feel the inner pulse of creedal statements as speech acts. The present one will survey the linguistic topography of these statements by setting them off from the statements of other forms of discourse and by pointing out those characteristics which relate them to these other forms. This will be done by fixing an ever sharpening focus on creedal statements relating them first to human language as a whole, then distinguishing them from the various uses of language and finally singling them out from other religious uses of language.

I. *Creedal Statements Linked with Everyday Language*

There are many ways by which man communicates with his fellowmen - by words, symbols, gestures. The most common way in which man consciously makes something known to another is by means of words, oral or written. This system of communication which is the special prerogative of man is called language.[1]

Creedal statements must be seen first of all in the context of human language. Just as language itself is imbedded in the human conditions of life, so are creedal statements in human language. The personal and social aspects of the creed which have been shown in the preceding section find anchorage in the essential "personalness" and "socialness" of language as such. Dallas High is at pains to point out that language can fulfill its function of communication only because of the "fiduciary acts" and "tacit understandings" presupposed in interpersonal relationships.[2] All forms of discourse share in these presuppositions. Even in philosophical arguments,

---

1 Cf. "Sprachphilosophie" in *Das Fischer Lexikon: Philosophie*, 9th ed. I, 308.

2 Dallas High, *Language, Persons and Belief*, 107 ff.

not all the claims of the discussants are self-evident and if one would have to verify for oneself every factual claim that enters into the premisses of the argument, no discussion would ever take place. The partners must have a minimum of reliance on each other's words. In scientific explanations, the ordinary layman or even an individual scientist cannot ascertain all the claims of the explanation by himself. He must rely on the statements of his collaborators or those who have worked before him. The creedal statement, although it has some other distinctive features, is basically grounded on the ordinary human mode of locution.

Language is constituted by areas of discourse which overlap with one another but which have enough distinct features to be recognized as specific areas of discourse. There is the everyday language, the professional and technical language of the sciences, both human and natural, the language used for religious purposes, for entertainment, etc. This does not mean that entirely different sets of words and word combinations are used for each type of discourse (except perhaps for constructed language models and highly formalized technical languages in the mathematical sciences) but rather, the same words or almost the same words with the help of technical terms particular to each form of discourse, are used in different contexts, in different areas of human experiences and investigations. In these specific areas, meanings of words may change; a combination of words can become a totally different speech act and therefore communicate a different linguistic force from that which the same combination of words would communicate in another area of discourse. For example, "I love you" said in an ordinary situation of human encounter has a different linguistic force from "I love you" said on a stage as a part of a drama.

The area that seems to spread widest in the map of human language is the so-called everyday or ordinary language. It is not easy to define what everyday or ordinary language is, because one cannot make a clear-cut separation between it and other types of discourse which it penetrates, or rather which it includes. For example, when two scientists are discussing at a conference banquet, where does scientific discourse stop and where does ordinary table-talk begin? The social small talk that is inevitable in such banquets is bound to be interspersed with serious discussions of scientific problems. Here, the term "everyday" language will be used to mean the type of discourse engaged in everyday human encounters, in the ordinary business of living. (Umgangssprache) It is what man uses as a member of the widest social group as contrasted to that which he uses in his professional life and which distinguishes him as a member of a smaller social group.

The immediate task is to relate creedal statements with everyday language by comparing and contrasting it with some language games of ordinary discourse such as "expressing one's belief," "stating one's knowledge," "promising," "expressing trust and confidence," "praising," and "making a pledge or a vow." There are of course countless other language games in human discourse, but only those which have some common, *prima facie* grounds for comparison/contrast with creedal discourse, are discussed here.

1. Expression of Belief

The discussion will begin with belief statements in general. In these kinds of statements, the main term is, of course, the verb "believe." Valuable to the analysis of the different belief utterances in everyday language is Dallas High's list of the typical uses of the verb "believe" which is summarized below:[3]

    a) Believe: (trust)
        i. a person. Ex. "I believe in Jones." meaning "I believe Jones is telling the truth" or "I trust Jones."
        ii. a form of speech or words. Ex. "I believe every word of it."
    b) Believe in, on, upon: (trust in, have faith in, have confidence in)
        i. a person. Ex. "I believe in Jones." meaning "I have confidence in Jones."
        ii. a form of speech or words, a statement or doctrine. Ex. "I believe in what you say."
        iii. a thing generally, e.g. in an institution, practise, idea, object. Ex. "I believe in democracy." "I believe in daily exercise."
    c) Believe that: accept that, agree that, have the opinion that. Ex. "I believe that it will rain." "I believe that Nixon is winning."

---

3 *Ibid.*, 147.

This list is not meant to be exhaustive but to bring home the point that belief statements are not to be limited to just one paradigm, i.e. "believe that," but that they can perform different functions. In Austinian terms, they can have different illocutionary forces.

The next paragraphs will show how religious creedal statements can be aligned with similar belief statements in everyday language. The first article of the Apostles' Creed, "I believe in God the Father Almighty" is an expression of trust and confidence similar to the statement "I believe in Mother Gertrud" or "I believe in Ralph Nader (the zealos fighter for consumer rights in America)." The three statements presuppose the reality of a God the Father, a Ralph Nader, a Mother Gertrud, whom one believes in, but *it is not* the primary intention of the statements to assert the existence of anyone. Rather, all three are expressive of trust and confidence. "I believe in God the Father Almighty" is similar to "I believe in Ralph Nader" in the sense that one affirms the doings of both - in the Father's acts of providence and in Ralph Nader's efforts to give consumers their due. Both also have the nuance of an expression of *praise*. It is like saying, "praised be Jahwe!" and "Hurrah, Ralph!" The same creedal statement "I believe in God the Father Almighty" shares a nuance with "I believe in Mother Gertrud" not shared by the first comparison, namely *personal trust*, which is brought out by the personal modification "Father" "Mother." One can believe in the act of another and praise him without believing or trusting in him as a person. The second comparison being expressive of personal relation, implies personal *commitment* to the person one trusts. For example faith in Mother Gertrud can commit one to following her advice in specific situations. Likewise, an expressed trust in God the Father can commit one to undergo a difficult ordeal, like for example, martyrdom.

A final note in the distinction of the creedal statement "I believe in God the Father Almighty" to the other two statements "I believe in Mother Gertrud" and "I believe in Ralph Nader" by the totality of the trust and commitment it expresses, because the object of trust in the first statement is qualified as "almighty."

The article of the creed, "I believe in the holy, catholic Church," is both like the statement, "I believe in democracy", i.e. having trust in an institution (b, iii. in High's list) and the statement, "I believe in Marxism" in the sense of trusting its principles. (a, ii.) In the first instance, the trust is on the effectiveness of the organization as a whole; it expresses one's sense of belonging to it as distinct from other institutions. In moments of persecution, it may mean a kind of casting one's lot with it, making its destiny one's own, just as in the critical situation in Germany in 1934, "I believe in democracy" could have meant the same kind of commitment to democracy as an institution. In the second instance, in comparison with "I believe in Marxism," one expresses faith in the veracity of what the Church teaches or in the authenticity of what she practices.

"I believe in the forgiveness of sins" and "I believe in life everlasting" both express a nuance of hope rather than just of an acceptance or agreement. "Forgiveness of sins" and "life everlasting" are neither persons nor experiences that one can ascertain by evidence or by ordinary human means. Therefore believing in them cannot have the nuance of trusting in persons as was in the first article of the creed. Rather, they are expressions of hope in the realization of certain desirable states, i.e. state of righteousness and a state of unending bliss anchored in some other creedal statements that "God the Father Almighty" and that "Christ saved us from our sins." But there is a slight difference between the two. The belief in life everlasting is exclusively future oriented. One hopes for something to come. The belief in the forgiveness of sins has the nuance of an expression of certainty that the sins one has committed in the past have been forgiven, but this certainty is founded on hope rather than on evidence. The hope element comes in again in the assurance that given the possibility of future sins, there is the trust that they too will be forgiven.

The Christological statements in the creed: "... and in Jesus Christ, our Lord... born of the Virgin Mary... suffered under Pontius Pilate, was crucified, died and was buried" although similar in their surface grammar to "I believe that Julius Caesar crossed the Rubicon" are not really expressing just a historical reliance but have in addition the trust-confidence force of the first article of the creed, namely, trust in the person of Christ and in his redemptive act.

This brief analysis shows that although the articles of the creed are strung along the same grammatical construction and written in the same indicative mood linked to each other by the same verb, "believe," they are not to be interpreted according to one paradigm but according to the multiform functions of the verb. From this analysis, one also sees that the functions of "believe" in creedal statements are active - as Dallas High puts it, "they are intentional placings by human beings" not mere "behavioral or mental dispositions to act in a certain way" or "something utterly given to a passive recipient."[4]

Belief statements, in their religious uses are not a reporting of one's mental state. They are commissive speech acts. They are to be differentiated from one type of use of "believe" in ordinary language as in the following context:

    John: "Do you think it will rain today?"

    Mary: "I believe so."

In this example, "believe" is used as an expression of an uncertain opinion. This is what Mats Furberg calls the "degree-showing" use of "believe," that means, it serves to show what degree of reliance the hearer is to place on the utterance.[5] Neither is the religious use of "I believe" identical with the delusional employment of the verb in the statement: "I believe him to be honest." By these contrasts we see a difference between the creedal use of the verb and some uses of it which in ordinary language are contrasted to the verb "I know." This brings the discussion to the relation of "I believe" to "I know."

    2. Expression of Knowledge

It is not the task here to put forward theories of knowledge but merely to investigate how the everyday use of "I know" is similar or distinct from the religious use of "I believe." There is a wider gap between the degree-showing, ordinary use of "I believe" with the everyday use of "I know" than there is between the religious use of "I believe" and the ordinary use of "I know." In ordinary language, one says, "I don't know, but I believe so," or "I don't only believe, I know!" These examples show a gap between uncertainty and certainty. Whereas in the religious use of "I believe," there is a conviction which is expressive of certainty expressed likewise by "I know." As Pieper writes: "It is a part of the concept of belief (religious) itself that a man is certain of that in which he believes."[6] In other words

---

4 *Ibid.*, 156.

5 Mats Furberg, *Saying and Meaning*, 233.

6 Josef Pieper, *Belief and Faith* tr. by R. and C. Winston (New York: Pantheon, 1963), 15.

"the assent implied in belief is as strong as in knowledge: It appears without reservation."[7] And when one takes into account the greater risks that people make on their beliefs, one can say that the degree of certainty is greater in the expression of one's belief in a religious context than in the statement of one's knowledge. Belief in a religious statement is opposed to evidence and not to the certainty of knowledge.

Dallas High characterizes the linguistic performance of religious creedal statements as "self-involving." They are giving answers not to questions of fact, but to some other questions. He explains further:

> The questions behind the creeds are self-involving questions, like the relation, loyalty, trust or value I may place in another person or something personalized... They are asking about the valuation of personhood like promises or covenants and are concerned about loyalty to another person or being who is like a person "I".[8]

This brings in the relation of "I believe" to "I promise," "I pledge," and "I vow."

3. Promise-Vow-Pledge Statements

How is the religious use of "I believe" to be compared to the verbs, "promise," "pledge," "vow"? The first thing one notices is that all the statements: "I believe," "I promise," "I vow," "I pledge," are performative in the earlier Austinian sense of not merely stating but actually doing what one is expressing. All are commissive. The person saying "I believe" in a religious context and the ordinary uses of the three other verbs are in one sense the same kind of speech act, although the commissive force of "I believe" is lesser than in the case of the other three. It appears that as speech acts of binding oneself, these verbs exhibit an increasing degree of binding force when they are aligned in the following order: "I believe," "I promise," "I pledge," "I vow." There is however an aspect where the first statement differs as a speech act from the other three. The felicity of the last three statements is necessarily connected with some future action on the part of the speaker. In the case of the belief statement, no future action is explicitly expressed, even if the subsequent behaviour of the speaker will show if he was honest in his utterance. A belief statement

---

7 M. Martin, *Varieties of Unbelief* (New York: Holt, Rinehart and Winston, 1964), 19.

8 High, *Op. Cit.*, 176.

differs therefore from the promise-pledge-vow utterances in that it is an expression of conviction or trust which implies commitment, while the latter three are acts of explicit commitment which imply conviction and trust. In the one case, the behabitive force is dominant and in the latter case, the commissive.

There is , however, a logical affinity between the types of speech acts contrasted above. The pledge-promise-vow statements presuppose belief in its aspect of trust - trust on the part of the person being promised to and trustworthiness on the part of the person promising. On the other hand, belief implies the fidelity aspect of a promise, pledge or vow. This affinity is especially exemplified in the covenant relations between Israel and Jahwe. This relation was a dynamic interaction of promise and belief utterances and situations. The Christian belief situation being rooted in the New Bond (Testament) is no less characterized by this interaction. Confronted with what they consider the divine promising and experiencing the fidelity of Jahwe in the fulfillment of the promises, the people of God express their trust in the God they thus experience by committing themselves to him by pledges and vows of fidelity.

II. *Creedal Statements Compared with Non-religious Uses of Language*

The complexity of human life occasions a corresponding complexity in human communication - in human language, or to be more exact, in the various uses of it. Thus we have scientific, philosophical, literary, aesthetic, ethical, political, etc. uses of language. The concern of this section is to delineate this use of language in relation to the other uses mentioned above. The different areas of discourse treated in this section are themselves made up of varying language games on a smaller scale. For example, the ethical discourse includes giving rules and following them, judging an action right or wrong, commanding and obeying, allowing and forbidding, etc. It cannot be expected that the creedal statement will be contrasted or compared with all conceivable language games of an area of discourse. There are some language games in these areas that do not touch creedal statements one way or the other. Another thing to note from the outset is that the religious use of language does not convert the status of its utterances to some esoteric level of linguistic understanding. It rather means that "certain grammatical contexts employ specifically religious concepts, concepts that have a semantic history, have meaning within communities and groups and are used to evoke responses characteristic of what is traditionally called religious behaviour."[9]

1. Scientific Discourse

The first non-religious use of language to which religious creedal statements will be compared is the scientific form of discourse[10] which is here limited to natural science. The scientific use of language is constituted by several language games such as reporting on observations of a natural phenomenon, forming and testing hypotheses, presenting the results of an experiment in tables and diagrams, etc. We limit the discussion here to the reporting of observations of natural phenomena and the forming and testing of a hypothesis.

With regard to the first, a ground of comparison must be looked for and this is done by recognizing that creedal statements do give a kind of information. But it must be strongly stated from the outset that creedal statements do not do so primarily. They are as speech acts behabitive and commissive expressions rather than constative or expositive statements such as scientific statements primarily are. Nevertheless as shall be shown in Chapter V, they do include cognitive informative content. Scientific statements, in reporting observations, aim at communicating empirical facts or explanation of these facts for the purpose of enhancing knowledge or understanding the physical world. Creedal statements on the other hand, first of all, do not give reports about observations. They give non-empirical "information"; they make assertions and claims. Even in cases when the subject matter of creedal statements coincides with scientific talk, i.e. about the material universe, the concern of the creedal statement is not to impart empirical explanations of empirical phenomena, but rather to relate these to a primarily religious concern - salvation. Belief talk is not primarily interested in provoking cognitive assent which it does not, however, exclude but presuppose. Its interest lies not in the quiddity of things but in their significance to a whole set of non-empirical values based on non-empirical presuppositions. This interest in life significance makes itself felt in the way religious belief talk expresses itself. As

---

9 Richard Bell, "Wittgenstein and Descriptive Theology," 6.

10 Cf. Karl Rahner, "Science as 'Confession'?" in *Theological Investigations*, III (Baltimore: Helicon Press, 1967), 385-400.

Bochenski remarks in the following, it is much closer to ordinary discourse than scientific discourse can ever be:

> ... the discourse of science especially when it is highly developed, is constructed, so to speak, autonomously, that is, without taking other discourse into consideration. A physicist, for example, does not need, while constructing a system, to take into consideration the everyday discourse he uses outside science. But the situation in RD (religious discourse) is different. RD is very closely connected with the TD (total discourse) ... that is, it cannot be disconnected and considered separately from the PD (profane discourse) of the same subject.[11]

In connection with the scientific activity of forming hypotheses, a common ground between scientific discourse and the theological form of creedal discourse is disclosed, namely, in their use of models. Here an attempt will be made to examine the use of the models in these two forms of discourse and see points of convergence and points of divergence between scientific and theological models. Scientific theories are usually accompanied by models such as valency bonds, atomic system, corpuscular and wave models, ether, phlogiston, etc. Religion talks in terms of Father, King, Shepherd, heaven, hell, life everlasting, sanctifying grace, etc.

A preliminary investigations of the models used in both forms of discourse shows that the scientific models are structural and pictorial in nature, whereas those of theology are more anthropomorphic and parabolic, i.e. they are constituted by anthropomorphically immediate images and epistemologically vivid stories. This gives an insight into the impulse behind the use of models in both forms of discourse. Science aims at making abstract reality concrete, while theology wishes to make immanent its transcendental concepts.

Frederick Ferré in his article, "Mapping Out the Logic of Models in Science and Theology"[12] points out some similarities and differences between scientific models and theological models. As the first common feature, he points out that both kinds of models serve to simplify the data at hand "to a form in which the mind can grasp them." (p.88) In other words, both

---

11 J. Bochenski, *The Logic of Religion* (New York: University Press, 1965), 58.

12 F. Ferré, "Mapping Out the Logic of Models in Science and Theology" in Dallas High, *New Essays in Religious Language*, 54-96.

are a help towards a greater degree of understanding. Secondly, both the
scientist and the theologian are conscious that the models they use are
not the same thing as what they model. Thus the scientist insists that its
models are always open to revision, and the *via negativa* of theology is
a way of underlining the fact that its affirmation fall short of the reality being talked about. But here divergent features already come into view.

Theology is more closely bound up with its models than scientific theories are in theirs. In Ferré's words: "Theology is much more dependent on
its models, particularly on the key composite biblical models of ultimate
reality, for the very statement of distinctively theological dimensions of
meaning and belief." (p.91) Any act of cognitive consent to creedal claims
has a necessary reference to its model of reality. That is why theological
models are more resistant to change than scientific models, although the
interpretation of these models do undergo change in the light of further
reflection and increasing knowledge. Perhaps an example will make this
clear. The model "hell" in the creedal statement "he descended into hell"
has survived through centuries, at least in the English version of the creed,[13]
but there have been various interpretations of it offered by theologians
down the ages, i.e. as the underworld, limbo, the realms of the dead, as the
place of the damned.

In contrast, scientific models are altered, discarded and replaced with
relatively little compunction. What are resistant to change in Science are
its theories. For example, the atomic theory has seen a veritable genalogy
of models. This interesting reversal, i.e. the permanence of theological
models and the transiency of its "hypotheses" concerning these models and
the transiency of scientific models and the tenacity of its theories, is
due to the difference in scope of the two kinds of models. Theological models have a more unlimited scope; they are "weltanschaulich" in character,
whereas scientific models are limited in scope; they picture single theories
or the logical structure of single phenomena. Furthermore, scientific models are empirically falsifiable. They can be proved inaccurate or ineffective by further experimentation, as Ferré rightly observes:

---

13 In some other versions, for example in German, a new translation expresses it as "hinabgestiegen in das Reich des Todes", translated, it
would read in English, "descended into the realms of death."

> Nothing stands in the way *in principle* of observing directly the
> molecule of gases that are now modeled as little elastic pellets
> like billiard balls. Perhaps more powerful electron microscope
> will one day permit a point for point comparison of billiard balls
> and simple molecules. Then the scientist will know just how accu-
> rate or how inaccurate his models have been. And he will need this
> billiard ball model far less than before. (p. 90 f.)

But such empirical testings of theological models are not on hand which makes them less prone to being discarded. Of course they are not absolutely resistant to change, because world views also change. But these changes are the outcome of a gradual process. They are more like erosion than explosion - a gradual process in which they are not really disproved but rather quietly abandoned.[14]

To summarize: As speech acts, creedal statements and scientific statements differ fundamentally in that creedal statements in their primary aspect are expressions of commitment, adherence or hope, while scientific statements are descriptions, explanations or predictions. Thus an act of confessing one's belief even when using a thousand-year-old formula has an element of spontaneity not present in scientific statements which are more objectively disinterested and impersonal in character. An aspect of creedal discourse, namely its cognitive-informative aspect touches the same level of speech act as the scientific information but only to be distinguished from it in its concern and the kind of "information" it gives. Finally, in its theological form, creedal discourse resembles scientific discourse in its use of models. Again there are significant differences, first in the impulse for using models, which influences the kind of models used and the way the models work. Thus notwithstanding the points in which they are similar, it has been sufficiently shown that the creedal and the scientific discourse are indeed distinct forms of discourse.

2. Philosophical Discourse

In its non-empirical concern, philosophical discourse comes closer to religious belief talk than the scientific discourse. There is not one kind of philosophical use of language. Here the religious belief talk will be related to logical and metaphysical discourses as representatives of the philosophical use of language.

---

14 F. Ferré, *Op. Cit.*, Footnote 79, p. 93.

In what way is a religious argument similar or distinct from a logical argument? Take as examples the following:

Logical argument: All men are mortal.

Peter is a man.

Peter is mortal.

Religious argument: When my child was sick, I prayed to God.

God heard my prayer.

I believe that God is the Almighty Father.

In the logical argument, there is an automatic progression. If one substitutes symbols "x, y, z," for the terms, the argument remains valid. The statements are linked to each other with a force of necessity. The conclusion necessarily flows from its premises. The argument is objective, impersonal, mechanical. In the religious argument, the premises have deep-rooted presuppositions - they are rooted in the whole biography of the person making the statements. There is no strict deductive process that links the statements together. The argument claims no absolute objective validity, but it is bound to the person uttering it and the circumstances in which it is uttered. The conclusion does not flow necessarily from the premises, rather the premises give "good grounds" for the conclusion. The religious argument is not so much illogical as a-logical.[15] Within a given context and presupposition, it can make a claim on human reason to understand it, but not with the force of logical necessity. The religious belief argument has a decisional, self-committing force which the logical argument does not have.

Metaphysical statements are often mixed up or identified with religious statements. Both seem to be talking about the same phenomenon; both are preoccupied with the transcendent and the ultimate. What is the difference, for example, between the statements: "Being is absolute Truth, Good, and Beauty," and "Christ is the Way, the Truth, and the Life?" The surface grammar can tempt one to make an equation of identity. But the depth grammar shows a divergence. The *is* in the first statement is an "is" of identification. The metaphysical statement is tautologous. In the religious statement, the "is" is predicative. Furthermore the concepts "way, truth and

---

15 L. Wittgenstein, "Lectures and Conversations," 57.

life" in the religious statement are not autonomous - way, truth, life for whom? - for me, for us, for mankind, for those who wish to be saved. Metaphysical statements claim to be answers to a theoretical enquiry concerning ultimates. Religious statements are not primarily concerned with making theoretical enquiries or answering them. Even in its interrogatory form, "Lord, why do you allow innocent children to die in wars?" or "Oh God, how patient can you be with men's stupidities?", a religious expression is not an enquiry but at most a rhetorical question, and more frequently an exclamation, a cry, an expression of dispair, a reproach or a praise or an expression of wonderment. Creedal statements do not claim a-priori validity as metaphysical claims do. Some creedal claims of a historical nature are subject to historical verifiability. Other creedal non-empirical claims, in spite of all attempts to prove them to be metaphysical necessities, have not been satisfactorily proven to be so. They are rather credible presuppositions which one can accept or reject.

Metaphysical concepts may be used as religious concepts, but a religious utterance using these same concepts becomes an utterly different speech act. It acquires explicitly illocutionary forces, whereas a metaphysical statement can at most have a perlocutionary force which it does not primarily intend but which may be effected by the force of the concepts it asserts. For example, the metaphysical statement on the oneness of Being can effect in an impressionable philosophy student a sense of solidarity with the things around him.

Finally, as articulations of two different human activities, namely believing and reflecting, the religious belief discourse and the philosophical discourse in general differ in still another aspect, namely in the social aspect of creedal religious discourse. Ratzinger characterizes the individual nature of philosophizing thus: "Philosophie ist ihrem Wesen nach das Werk des einzelnen, der als einzelner die Wahrheit bedenkt."[16] In contrast, believing and the expression of belief in a religious context presupposes a community of faith where one gives witness, and with whom one shares one's beliefs. Ratzinger, following this same line of thought, continues:

---

16 J. Ratzinger, *Einführung in das Christentum*, 63.

> Der Vollzugsraum des Gedankens ist der Innenraum des Geistes; so
> bleibt er zunächst auf mich beschränkt, hat individualistische
> Struktur. Erst sekundär wird er mitteilbar, wenn er ins Wort ge-
> bracht wird, das ihn freilich meist nur annähernd dem anderen er-
> faßbar macht. Im Gegensatz dazu ist... für den Glauben das Primäre
> das verkündigte Wort. Während der Gedanke innerlich, bloß geistig
> ist, stellt das Wort das Verbindende dar. Es ist die Weise, wie im
> Geistigen Kommunikation entsteht, die Form, wie der Geist gleich-
> sam menschlich ist, das heißt leibhaftig und sozial. Dieser Primat
> des Wortes besagt damit, daß Glaube in einer ganz anderen Weise als
> philosophisches Denken auf Gemeinschaft des Geistes hingeordnet ist.[17]

But the preceding reflections do not deny that creedal discourse has something to do with logic and metaphysics. Creedal statements have a kind of logic, first, in the sense that they cannot bear contadictions within one and the same statement and among the statements within the system of the Christian religious discourse. In a creedal statement, concepts that are logically compatible are combined. Even the statement on the Trinity is not a matter of 3 = 1, but it qualifies 3 as "persons" and 1 as "nature." Within the system, there might be paradoxes but not downright contradictions. Creedal statements have also a certain kind of coherence, but here again the coherence differs from that of formal logic. In a logical syllogism, the conclusion is coherently drawn from the premisses. The coherence of creedal statements is more like the coherence in Art. It is a structural coherence, a coherence of patterns. For example in a mosaic picture, the fitting of a piece to the whole pattern is not a matter of logical deduction but a matter of a sense of harmony or wholeness. In a similar manner, the dogma of the Assumption is not a logical deduction from any of the primary articles of the creed. It is coherent to them in the context of the whole Christian tradition and of the role of Mary in Catholic spirituality throughout the ages. It is quite understandable for people looking at it from other perspectives not to see its point. But even if the type of consistency or coherence in logic differs from that in belief, all coherence and consistency finally depend on one common bedrock, namely, the consistency of life itself.[18]

Religious creedal talk is likewise related to metaphysical discourse

---

17 *Loc. Cit.*

18 Cf. L. Wittgenstein, *Remarks on the Foundation of Mathematics*, German with English translation by G.E.M. Anscombe, ed. by G.H. von Wright and R. Rhees and G.E.M. Anscombe (Oxford: Basil Blackwell, 1956).

taken to mean discourse about trans-empirical realities. In fact, as has been mentioned earlier, many creedal assertions are in the realm of metaphysical reality using meta-physical concepts. In short: Creedal statements share a common ground with metaphysics in the transcendence of their referents, but as speech acts, creedal discourse differs from the reflective systematic discourse of the philosophical discipline known as Metaphysics.

3. Ethical Discourse

In the face of logical positivistic attack on religious belief statements, some recent philosophers of religion have tried to reduce or to identify religious discourse with ethical discourse so as to save it from the embarrassment of verifying its assertions which the positivists had declared to be impossible.[19] To save the religious creedal statement from the verdict of "meaninglessness," these philosophers tried to show that the creedal assertions are not really assertions - that they are not cognitive. Rather they are conative or imperative. They are moral resolutions.[20] This is a very understandable attempt at "saving" religious belief talk, because there is indeed an overlapping between the two forms of discourse. There are no clear-cut boundary lines between them. The self committing force of religious belief statements does give an ethical coloring to the statement. It expresses at least a readiness to act in a certain way compatible to the way of life one assents to and to avoid actions that go contrary to its principles. Much of religious belief talk is evaluative. Adherence to persons and principles presuppose that one sees value in them. Furthermore belief utterances have a character of first person imperatives similar to resolutions and pledges. But in spite of all these, belief statements cannot be reduced to ethical statements.

Belief talk is self-committing, because it relies on a presupposition which justifies, calls for and even effects commitment. It relies on its constative assertive aspects, on its theistic and Christological presuppositions which are not necessary for ethical statements but are indispensible

---

19 Cf. A.J. Ayer, *Language, Truth and Logic*.

20 This is the main argument of Braithwaite's "An Empiricist's View of the Nature of Religious Belief."

for the religious belief utterance. There are, of course, ethical statements within religious discourse, but then these have as their basis some belief statements. For example, the Catholic ruling on divorce is based on a creedal affirmation of the sacramentality of marriage.

As speech acts, creedal statements are primarily behabitive-commissive in force, while ethical talk being primarily evaluative is more verdictive-exercitive, i.e. it judges the value or disvalue of acts and prescribes right actions for certain situations. However, it must be pointed out that notwithstanding their differences as speech acts, creedal statements and at least the Christian form of ethical discourse complement one another. Creedal utterances, if honest, must flow into moral commitment. Christian moral discourse in contrast to other forms of ethical discourse relies on religious presuppositions and sanctions to be effective. This will be treated more fully in a separate section on moral religious discourse.

4. Aesthetic Discourse

Another reductionistic theory concerning religious discourse is apt to identify it with aesthetic discourse. Let us reflect on some examples of this type of discourse to see how near they come to creedal religious discourse thus understanding the tendency to identify them with this, as well as to see in what ways they differ as to warrant their being taken as two distinct forms of discourse.

There are many kinds of "beauty talk" but two which come invariable to mind when the term "Aesthetics" is mentioned are the reflective philosophical kind and Art critique. The comparison will be limited to these two forms of aesthetic discourse. An example of the philosophical type is a paragraph chosen at random in a dissertation on transcendental aesthetics:

> "Das Schöne im allgemeinen muß auf der einen Seite das ganz Endliche auf der anderen zugleich die unmittelbare Gegenwart der Idee sein." Das bedeutet: Das Schöne kann einerseits nie schön sein ohne die Gegenwart der Idee, andererseits kann das Schöne nicht unabhängig von der Erscheinung bestehen, weil es der sinnlichen Wahrnehmung gegeben wird und damit ganz Erscheinung ist. Das Schöne soll also sich als Erscheinung "mitten in Widersprüchen schön erhalten," es "schwebt frei in der Mitte zwischen Gemeinem und Göttlichem."[21]

---

[21] Masako Odagawa, *Oskar Becker's phänomenologische Aesthetik*, Doctoral dissertation, (Würzburg: Julius Maximilian Universität, 1970), 50.

Of the critical type, there are sometimes simple descriptive phrases like: "A painting uses pale colors, predominantly blue and green and has kneeling figures on the foreground," or "The theme of the fugue is inverted at such a point and there is a stretto at the close." But usually these straightforward descriptions, which are easily understandable to men with normal senses and intelligence are only preparatory to the real evaluative phrases which would require the exercise of taste, perceptiveness, sensitivity of aesthetic descrimination or appreciation for their understanding. Examples are: "The picture lacks balance." "It has a certain serenity and repose." "The grouping of the figures set up an exciting tension."

In comparison with the philosophical aesthetic discourse, creedal religious discourse may perhaps share in the sublimity of subject matter. In this sense, both are not "thing-language." However, the creedal discourse is much nearer to the concerns of ordinary human living than aesthetic discourse, which is more speculative in character. The creedal discourse, having existential concerns, exhibits behabitive-commissive forces; the philosophical aesthetic discourse being more reflective, is primarily constative and expositive. Philosophical easthetics contemplates beauty and reveals its characteristics in a disinterested objective manner. Creedal religious discourse asserts and claims certain attributes about persons and significance of events which cannot be arrived at just by reflection on the person or events but must be rejected or accepted on the strength of testimony.

In comparison with the critical aesthetic discourse, there are some creedal statements which resemble the simple straightforward attribution of qualities which Art critique makes. And like the descriptions of Art critique, these statement point to a significance beyond themselves. The difference lies first in that the descriptive attributions of Art critique speak of something perceived by the senses, whereas creedal attributions are either of something trans-empirical or something of the past or the future but rarely of something present to the senses. It is quite a different language game to be describing what one sees or hears or what one has seen or heard, from that of recalling events that have **happened** thousands of years ago, or from asserting or claiming something about trans-empirical realities or from pledging oneself to someone or from expressing assent to some truth claim on the strength of testimony - all of which belong to the language game of creedal discourse. And the significance to which aesthetic statements point is of a different kind from that to which creedal statements call attention. Artistic significance appeals only to a part of man, religious significance involves man's whole existence.

Compared to the evaluative critical aesthetic discourse, the creedal discourse appears to be more straightforward and more ordinary in the style of its formulation. One does not need a special "religious taste" to understand at least what they claim. It takes perhaps more to accept them, but even the unbeliever can make something of what they state. Whereas one must at least have a minimum of artistic sensitivity to understand what it means for a painting to be "full of tension," or for a passage of music to be "sparkling." Perhaps this is due in part to the difference in impulse behind a creedal statement and the aesthetic statement. The creedal statement is, as has been often said throughout this work, impelled by a need to express assent to a truth claim, to stand up to one's conviction, to express one's attitude or commitment to someone or something, all in the context of religious concern, such as salvation, forgiveness, seeing a meaning in life, etc. The aesthetic discourse is an interpretative linguistic articulation which aims at sharing the observer's insight and to evoke the same understanding or mood provoked by a word of art, or of nature, or of something beautiful. Art critique does this by isolating and placing in a frame of attention, the particular feature of an object which makes it beautiful or ugly. For this, aesthetic discourse uses a vocabulary evocative of pleasurable or non-pleasurable response such as "unified, balanced, serene, somber,etc." For a certain effect one also resorts to pressing into service words which do not primarily function in such a manner in their ordinary use, for example, the use of "violent" in describing color, the use of phrases such as "dancing lines," "tight-knit poem," "angry rhythm," etc. Hampshire calls this "an unnatural use of words in description."[22]

In contrast, creedal statements are less metaphorical and less arbitrary in their use of words. When metaphors are used, the effect intended is not so much the evoking of a mood, although this is not utterly excluded, but primarily the clarification or concretization of concepts.

---

22 Stuart Hampshire, quoted in Frank Sibley "Aesthetic Concepts" in *The Philosophical Review*, LXVIII (1959), 441.

Taking the two types of aesthetic discourse together, one sees that they both are evaluative in character, something which religious creedal discourse is not, at least not directly and primarily.

This makes aesthetic discourse object oriented. The focus of attention is on the object being descibed, interpreted or evaluated. It is detached in its appraisal. It is disinterestedly objective in its appreciation of beauty. The creedal discourse, on the other hand, is less objective and more self-involving. It is a decisional deliberation and is expressive of commitment to claims. The speaker is personally involved in what he says. Creedal discourse therefore speaks as much of the speaker as of what it speaks about. This characteristic of creedal discourse has been recognized by R.F. Holland in his essay, "Religious Discourse and Theological Discourse" which has been treated in Chapter I.[23] It is to be recalled that in that essay, Holland interprets the statements, "God is the Creator to whom one owes everything" and "God is the God of mercy of whose forgiveness we stand in need" as statements about God in the same sense that the statement "I owe my life to my parents" would be an assertion about the parents, i.e. they are much more statements about the speaker.

To summarize: As speech acts, creedal discourse and aesthetic discourse, though both speak of sublime matters and are concerned with "significance" are distinct forms of discourse. First, because they usually talk of different subject matters and even when they talk of the same thing, they are concerned with different types of significance, the aesthetic with artistic significance and the creedal discourse with religious significance. They also emit differing linguistic forces, the aesthetic discourse being primarily constative and in cases where it emits illocutionary forces, it is more of the verdictive type. The creedal discourse on the other hand exhibits primarily illocutionary forces, particularly the behabitive-commissive types.

5. Poetic Discourse

Closely related to aesthetic discourse is the poetic use of language. Poets are artists whose principal medium is the word. Since the Christian religious belief is located in the context of a word-revelation, it is to

---

23 Cf. R.F. Holland, "Religious Discourse and Theological Discourse," 49 f.

be expected that it can take expression in literary statements as well. Holy Scripture abounds in literary statements and real poetry. Written prayers are most often genuine poems. Religious language songs are poems set to music.

Creedal statements and poetry can be very similarly constructed. Compare:

Creedal statement: I believe in God the Father Almighty, Creator of heaven and earth.
I believe in Jesus Christ, his Only Son, Our Lord.

Verse: I believe that for every drop of rain that falls, a flower grows.
I believe that somewhere in the darkest night, a candle glows.

A grammatical diagram would show an overlapping structure. Depth grammar, however, shows some differences. The first point of difference is the existential importance of the creedal utterance. As Dallas High points out, "When we attend to the verb 'believe' (speaking of creedal statements), we come upon action and agency of performance even if it is only that action of 'expressing beliefs' - serious expressions as opposed to play-acting expressions..."[24] The utterance of a creedal statement can be a question of life and death as in the case of the martyrs. In a less dramatic situation, it can mean a whole orientation of life. It is an affirmation with consequences.

Poetry on the other hand, even when expressive of profound truths and deep insights akin to religious statements, has an "entertainment" aspect absent in the creedal utterance. In the *Encyclopedia Britannica*, we read:

> While being in some forms a "sacred" art or "mystery" associated with the practice of fertility and purification rituals, and with ideas of spiritual possession, it (poetry) seems also to have had recreational aspects. Even in its periods of greatest religious and magical significance it seems to have been regarded as a game to be played with words, an entertainment, passtime, and mode of personal emotional release.[25]

---

24 Dallas High, *Language, Persons and Belief*, 149.

25 "Poetry" in *Encyclopedia Britannica*, 1969, ed., vol. 18, 90-91.

Another element which distinguishes creedal statement from poetry is the same which has distinguished it from aesthetic discourse, namely its assertive character. The creedal statement is expressive of conviction or commitment to ascertain truth claims. To create a mood in others does not belong to its intentionality as a speech act. Poetry shares the intention of the aesthetic discourse to create such a mood and therefore shares its evocative language. Clive Samson writes: "Poetry is a rhythmical form of words which expresses an imaginative-emotional-intellectual experience of the writer and expresses it in such a way that it creates a similar experience in the mind of his reader or listener."[26] This explains why poetry is often written with the same arbitrary use of words as aesthetic discourse and in most cases it is even obscure in its surface grammar. A stanza from Thomas Dylan will exemplify this point. The first stanza of his poem, "Then Was My Neophyte" reads:

> Then was my neophyte
> Child in white blood bent on its knees
> Under the bell of rocks,
> Ducked in the twelve, disciple seas
> The winder of the water-clocks
> Calls a green day and night.[27]

The unusual combinations of concepts can be syntactically very confusing, but this extraordinary juxtaposition of carefully chosen imagery can provoke the mood or emotional reaction intended by the author. Poetic discourse consequently pays much attention to verbal dexterity which is not of much importance in the creedal discourse. Of course creedal statements can likewise be expressed in a poetic way, as for example the Athanasian Creed. But in this case, the literary form is used as a medium and style never takes precedence over the content. Even when written as a poem, there is no abandoning of one language game for another. Rather one remains in the language game of confessing one's belief but using another as vehicle of expression. The religious use of literary poetical statements is secondary and instrumental. Poetry is primarily and autonomously literary in the sense that it serves its own literary aims first before it

---

26 *Ibid.*, 91.

27 Dylan Thomas, "Then Was My Neophyte" in *Collected Poems, 1934-1952* (London: J.M. Dent and Sons, Inc., 1966), 63.

functions in some other role. A creed, even if written in bad poetry can be a "good" creed in the sense of possessing all the characteristics of such a speech act. On the other hand, a verse even if it can well serve some other purpose, may fail to be genuine poetry.

6. Political Discourse

Another area of discourse which may have some aspects to be contrasted or compared to creedal discourse is political discourse. Again this implies a variety of forms: campaign slogans, speeches, rallies, political harangue, etc. There seems to be quite an affinity between some creedal acclamations and political slogans. Both are expressive of commitment to a certain person or to a certain cause. They may be manifestations of loyalty to such a person or a cause. Compare: "Jesus is Lord!" and "Magsaysay is my guy!" Both may have the characteristic of being an index of belonging to a particular group, in the case of the creed to a religious group, in the case of the political slogan or manifesto to a particular political party.

The platform of a political party is a summary of its ideals and program in a similar way that the creed is the summary of the main tenets of the Christian faith community. The baptismal pledge of a convert expressing his allegiance by reciting the creed has the characteristic of a manifesto likewise expressed by the pledge of loyalty by members of the political party. In a political rally, the speeches usually have the past-present-future structure of the creeds. There is a recalling of the deeds done by a political candidate which are interpreted to be responsible for some present good and which then are offered as a pledge for his future service. Likewise in the creedal formula, there is an enumeration of salvific events to which the believer expresses adherence in the present and which he takes as a guarantee for his eschatological hopes.

But aside from the vast difference in concern of political discourse and creedal discourse, there are differences even in their character as speech acts. There is an element of "propaganda" in the political discourse which is not found in the religious creedal talk. Political talk primarily aims to persuade, to convince even to manipulate the hearers as is done by demagogues. The creedal statements are primarily expressions of belief and only secondarily a giving of witness or testimony. They do not principally aim to make converts. This is the principal function of another religious use of language, namely, missionary preaching. That is why eloquence is not necessary to a creedal statement as it is to political speeches. In Austinian terms, the creedal statement has a predominantly behabitive-commissive force in comparison to the political discourse which exhibits a strongly exercitive force.

III. *Creedal Statements Within Religious Discourse*

The analysis began by locating creedal statements within the broad field of human everyday language. Within this vast area, attention had been focused on the religious use of language by tracing the boundaries which separated it from other forms of discourse. Overlapping in some points was also shown. Within the area of religious discourse, the ever sharpening focus will finally be fixed on the main concern of this work - on creedal statements as distinguished from other forms of statements used in the religious context.

The religious use of language obviously does not exhaust itself in creedal statements. Language is used in the religious context to execute religious tasks. Dallas High lists among others - "to pray, to worship, to name a god or God, to prescribe action, to relate a myth or a story, to recount history, to sing the Nunc Dimittis, or to say creeds."[28]

The present task is to relate the creedal utterance with the other language games found in religious discourse, namely: praying and worshipping, prescribing actions, recounting history (of salvation), preaching, administering the sacraments, expressing theological reflections, and expressing mystical experiences.

1. Prayer and Worship

Prayer, which is a form of interpersonal relationship takes on varied forms due to the complexity of such a relationship. Thus there are prayers of praise and adoration, thanksgiving, contrition and petition. This personal aspect of prayer brings it close to creedal utterances. Its commissive (ex. I dedicate my life to you), behabitive (I praise you, I adore you) aspects are shared by creedal statements in their pledge and doxological character, especially when used in a liturgical context. The history of the traditional creeds shows that they had their *Sitz im Leben* in the

---

28 Dallas High, *Language, Persons and Belief*, 135.

worship of the early Church. Creedal formulae were used as acclamations and therefore as prayers of praise, adoration, and thanksgiving for the good news of salvation which they acclaimed. And yet it would be inaccurate to identify the creed with prayer, even if they have the same cognitive content or even if the very same creedal formula is used as a prayer. Creedal statements are in their primary intention, profession of faith. They are not primarily addressed to God but to the believing community or to a hostile crowd. That is why they do not take the vocative form which prayer almost always does.

There is also the essential public character of the creed as a testimony, which prayer does not necessarily have. Even if prayer is said in common, it can likewise be said alone in the deep recess of one's heart. But the creed used as a testimony requires an audience. Another characteristic of the creed in its synodal form is its juridical function which prayer never has. Prayer, in no form, makes legislations about a wrong or right kind of prayer. If there is such a norm for prayer, this norm would be outside the language game of praying. Furthermore, prayer does not necessarily assert or make truth claims as the creed does. Even if it mentions the same truth as the creed does, it is either to praise God for it, to thank God for it, or to ask God something about it.

To summarize: Creedal statement and prayer utterances are in their primary functions distinct forms of speech acts, but the creed in a secondary function can be used as a prayer. It is because of the breadth of the field that makes up what is called prayer that the creed may likewise be used as such. The relationship is, however, not reciprocal. The creed may be used as a prayer, but not every prayer can be used as a profession of faith.

2. The Language of Morals

Within religious discourse, there is a great deal of "prescribing action" statements. How is this language of morals to be related to the language of faith? There is no lack of philosophers who would identify the two. Braithwaite, for example, thinks that "I believe in God" is equivalent to "a resolution to live an agapeistic way of life."[29] Without making the same kind of reduction, D.Z. Phillips nevertheless points out the close

---

29 Braithwaite, *Op. Cit.*, 240.

relationship between the two: "To understand what it means to believe in God is to understand why must God must be obeyed."[30] But to establish this connection, it is necessary to make distinctions between the two. The "is" in Phillips does not identify moral judgements with faith judgements. Rather the moral judgement flows from the religious assent. The individual religious belief statement provides the cognitive content which serves as the criterion of moral judgement and as motivation for moral acts.

Religious belief talk is the cognitive framework within which moral discourse (as distinguished from ethical discourse) acquires its distinctive significance. Phillips writes: "Unlike morality which recognizes that sometimes it is not wrong to decide against one's obligations to one's father (ethics), religion (religious morals) recognizes no circumstances in which one is justified in deciding against one's obligation to God."[31]

Assent to the belief that "God is Father Almighty" is an assent to the whole way of life in which Christian moral discourse is to be located. But assent to God being Father Almighty is not in itself a moral judgement. Rather it is a belief statement which forms the horizon of a number of moral judgements. Moral discourse and actions, on the other hand, provide the gauge of the meaning and force of religious belief talk. They are an important aspect of the realization of the commissive force of belief statements. They provide in part the backing for the felicity of belief talk as performative statements in the original Austinian sense.

3. Narrative and Reporting Statements

Religious discourse contains likewise historical narratives, parables, myths, miracle reports, description of incidents. When one reads the traditional creeds, one find statements that do not differ from historical narratives, as for example the Christiological interpolation in the Apostles' Creed.

However, creedal statements, even if they have the same content as narratives about the history of salvation, are nevertheless a distinct form of speech act. Historical narratives are primarily descriptive and informative. The accent is on the constative act of the statements even if there are other intentions like edification, entertainment, clarification, or

---

30 D.Z. Phillips, *Faith and Philosophical Enquiry* (London: Routledge and Kegan Paul, 1969), 228.

31 *Ibid.*, 231.

exhortation. In historical narration, the personal conviction of the person reporting is not important. Of course the effectiveness of the report or narration may be influenced by the conviction of the narrator, but the emphasis is on the objective force of the events narrated to convince and not on the resolute will or even the personal conviction of the narrator. In fact a criterion for good reporting and historical narration is the degree of objectivity managed by the reporter or historian.

In contrast, observe the emphasis in the following creedal statement of St. Therese: "When I write... about the happiness of heaven and the eternal possession of God... I'm simply talking about what I'd determined to believe."[32] Of course this is just one type of creedal statement, the "hope type." But the point is that such an element can feel at home in the language game of creedal discourse but not in the more objective discourse of reporting and narrating. Creedal discourse rests on testimony, just as reporting and narrating do, but the creedal discourse makes the testimony its own; reporting and narrating present it for what it is worth without commitment to it.

Creedal statements, even if they have a cognitive content and can fulfill an informative function, as in the case of declaratory creeds, are not in their original character as speech acts informative. The synodal creeds also, of course, fulfill the function of telling the faithful what they should believe and confess, but this is a secondary function. The synodal creed is primarily the confession of faith of the bishops. The faithful at Mass reciting the creed together are not telling each other the same story or informing each other of the same events, but they are committing themselves to God in virtue of these events or assertions. The catechumen who rectes the creed before baptism is making an act of assent or pledge and not re-telling an information, although by the very act, the salvific events may be recounted.

The above reflections may account for the act that even if it is not ideal, one can say the creed in a foreign tongue one does not fully understand or in a thousand year old formula. But it is not possible to narrate or report an event except in a language one knows actually how to use. One

---

32 Therese of Lisieux, *Autobiography*, 257.

can, of course, learn a story in a foreign language by heart and re-tell it. But such a speech act is not ordinarily called "telling a story" but "reciting a memorized piece." Due to the tacit presuppositions and conventional agreement involved in the context of reciting a creed, the creedal utterance made in another tongue one does not ordinarily know to use is still an act of faith, provided that the other conditions for making an act of faith are present. That means, presupposing that one knows the contents of the creed in one's own tongue and knowing that reciting it in a certain context, i.e. at Holy Mass, means an act of confessing one's faith, then in reciting the creed in a foreign language, one performs the linguistic act of confessing one's belief with the same force as when one says it in one's own dialect.

4. Preaching and Catechizing

Another form of religious discourse which overlaps to some extent with narrating or reporting, is preaching or catechizing. Narration and stories are made use of in religious instruction or in sermons. As a speech act, however, preaching is not mainly expositive as a narration primarily is. Preaching and catechizing have a witness character which puts them closer to creedal utterances. When one preaches or teaches catechism, one is backing up one's statements. One is taken to be vouching for what one says. One is taking responsibility for one's claims. All of these are included but not necessary in telling a story. In this regard, preaching and catechizing have something in common with creedal utterance. It, too, vouches for what it asserts. It commits itself to its truth claims. And the truth claims it confesses are precisely the same that are preached in sermons and taught in catechetical instructions.

However, the classroom or the pulpit are not the natural habitat of the creed. The didactic aspect of preaching or catechizing is utterly foreign to the creed. If by its utterance, it "teaches" or "edifies," it does so only secondarily. Teaching or preaching on the other hand are primarily didactic. They aim at effecting something in others - in evoking some cognitive reactions in the hearers. The creedal statement is more of an expression. One can teach or preach without conviction, and the act, though perhaps poor and ineffective, can still be called teaching or preaching. But conviction belongs to the conditions necessary to the felicity of a creedal statement as a speech act.

5. Theological Discourse

The individual creedal statement, which is rooted in the traditional creedal formula, is the main concern of theological discourse. The question is: "What is the difference between a theologian's making a theological statement and his uttering a creedal statement?" A theologian making a theological statement can be presupposed to be uttering a statement he believes in, and yet this does not make his statement a creedal statement. Since in the perception and acceptance of revelation, a certain amount of reflection is involved, the creedal statement which is the original answer to revelation, may be said to be the first reflection on it. Theological statements would then be a second reflection, since they reflect on this first spontaneous reflective reaction to revelation. A creedal statement is primarily an act of affirmation. A theological statement has rather a critical, analytical, and prescriptive function. It exercises a critical function in that it judges the consistency and coherence of the statements within Christian religious discourse. It does this by analysing the human experience of the divine, the written records of these experiences, and the ever changing human situation in which these original experiences are supposed to have significance. It also at times decides what can be meaningfully said in religious discourse and formulates the standards for moral action. Theological discourse is thus more a reflective discourse while creedal discourse is more an expressive one.

Another distinguishing factor is the public character of the creedal discourse. The synodal creeds have indeed made use of theological reflection and have incorporated in their decrees theological statements. But in the act of proclamation of the council decree, these statements assume another character. They are no longer mere private reflections or opinions; they have been assimilated into the corporate belief of the community. As such they have become norms for further theological reflections. On occasions they are judgements rejecting other theologiacl positions. In other words, they differ still on another point with other private theological statements in that they assume an official juridical character.

6. Sacramental Formula

As a formula, the creed must also be compared to other religious formulae, as for example those used in the administration of the sacraments. As speech acts, both creedal and sacramental formulae possess more than just an expositive force. They do not describe any state of affairs, rather they perform by their utterance. This linguistic performance varies from one sacramental formula to the other. It is therefore necessary to relate the creedal formula not with sacramental formulae in general but with the individual ones. The creedal utterance and the form of Baptism are similar in that they are strictly performative, i.e. the act of saying a belief statement is an act of faith, just as the pronouncing of the words of the baptismal formula combined with certain actions constitute the act of baptizing. The sacramental pledge in Matrimony in the pronouncing of the marriage vows has a commissive force which the response of the catechumen to the interrogatory creed in his baptismal pledge also has. The formula of absolution and the "let him be anathema" of the synodal creeds both exhibit exercitive force. However, the "let him be anathema" of the synodal creed does not by itself effect the excommunication by the mere fact of the promulgation of the decree. It provides rather the normative ground for excommunication which in some cases is effected by a separate juridical act. The words of absolution on the other hand are strictly performative.

It may be said in general, that whatever the distinctive illocutionary force of each sacramental formula may be, these formula has the character and intention of effecting something on a third person or of creating some state of affairs. Creedal statements do not have such motives or powers. They are expressions, commissive-behabitive expressions of one's relation to someone or of one's stand on something. Moreover even in the type of creedal statement (synodal creed) where there is a decisional aspect or exercitive force, the state of affairs brought about is on another plane as the state of affairs the sacramental formulae claim to bring about. The synodal creed brings about a purely juridical state of affairs. But it does not claim to effect a change in reality, conceived in any sense. The case where a book is judged heretical after the promulgation of a conciliar decree is no exception. No reality is changed. What changes is the *evaluation* of reality.

Sacramental formulae, on the other hand, claim to effect what they utter in a realm that goes beyond the purely juridical, in the realm of reality, which for want of a better term we choose to call mystical reality. Here is where creedal discourse and sacramental discourse meet. Without the creedal affirmation of this realm of reality, the claims of sacramental formulae would make no sense. In Austinian terms, the exercitive force of the sacramental formula depends on the constative force of the creedal statement.

7. Mystical Language

The last form of discourse within religion with which creedal statements will be compared is the language of the mystics. A whole book can be devoted to the analysis of mystical language. Here the interest is on its statements about God and reality similar to creedal statements. In the writings of the mystics, one does come across assertions that are most similar to creedal statements. The subject matter of the articles of the creed - God, heaven, hell, eternal life, etc., can likewise be the subject matter of mystical utterances. But is a creedal utterance the same speech act as a mystical utterance?

A reflection on mystical language shows that even if it contemplates the same phenomenon which a creedal statement confesses, the mystical language resembles more the poetic and aesthetic forms of discourse than the creedal discourse. It is like them a communication of a state of mind rather than the decisional expression of conviction or commitment to a claim as creedal discourse is. It therefore also makes an un-prosaic use of language as poetic and easthetic discourse. It exhibits the same arbitrary combination of words as exemplified in its use of such contradictory phrases such as "dazzling obscurity," "soundless sounds," "whispering silence," which are reminiscent of poetry and Art critique. In addition, mystical language makes use of a language of identity with the Divine in a way never found in creedal discourse, but not unusual in poetry. From Angelus Silesius, one can find an example of this type of language:

> "Ich bin so gross als Gott
> Er ist als ich so klein;
> Er kann nicht über mich,
> Ich unter ihm sein."[33]

In contrast to mystical, poetic, and aesthetic discourses, creedal discourse is sober, straightforward and prosaic in its formulation and it uses the ordinary syntactical rules of language.

A very fundamental difference between creedal utterance and mystical

---

33 Angelus Silesius, quoted in William James, *Op. Cit.*, 415.

utterance is the public, communal character of the first. It is a sharing in the community of faith. Mystical utterance, even if it edifies a community, is essentially private. William James supports this contention thus: "Mystical truth exists for the individual who has the transport, but for no one else. It resembles the knowledge given to us in sensations more than that given by conceptual thought."[34] The affirmations of the creedal statements are, in contrast, not for an individual person but for a community of believers. Without this communal context, the speech act of confessing one's believe has no significance. Its claims are therefore communicable unlike the mystical transport which is characterized by its incommunicability.

But even if mystical discourse and creedal discourse differ as speech acts, they are not completely independent of each other. The creedal affirmations lie at the base of mystical experience at least of the Christian kind. They form the criterion which separates authentic mystical utterances from delirious mumblings.

8. Conclusion

In all these efforts to focus on creedal statements, one overwhelming observation made is the lack of facility in obtaining a sharp focus. Creedalstatements tend to overlap with the most of the language games of religious discourse. When one preaches, one uses creedal affirmations as subject matters. When one prays one mentions creedal truth claims. And what is catechetical instruction but an elaboration of the articles of the creed? Without the creed, theology will have no object of reflection.

Creedal statements permeate all the other forms of religious discourse, so that a characteristic which distinguishes a creedal statement from one form relates it to another and vice versa. For example, a creedal statement distinguishes itself from prayer statements by the importance of its truth claims, but these make it nearer to theological discourse, catechizing and preaching. The creedal utterance, however, differs from these by its expressive rather than reflective or didactic character, which brings it nearer to prayer. Its commissive force which distinguishes it from theological discourse brings it nearer to some sacramental formulae which in-

---

34 W. James, *Ibid.*, 420.

clude pledges or vows.

Creedal statements appear to be the main spring from which all the other religious uses of language flow. As has been said, they provide the subject matter for theological reflection, preaching and catechizing. Prayer draws its sentiments from the convictions of creedal affirmations. If one is not convinced that God is almighty and loving, there is no sense in prayers of petition and prayers of trust. The prayers of praise and thanksgiving are an acknowledgement of the creedal attribution of perfections to God and deeds of salvation to Christ. Prayer of contrition is pointless if there are no creedal assertions on sin, salvation and the mercy of God. Even mysticism would be mere gushings or at best literary expressions if not anchored on creedal truth claims.

The analysis, with all its difficulty in obtaining a sharp focus, at least points to this central role of creedal statements in the Christian religious discourse.

Chapter V

THE QUESTION OF "MEANING" AND "TRUTH" REGARDING CREEDAL STATEMENTS

In Chapter III, the inner dynamic of creedal statements has been shown by examining their uses, purposes and functions in the different contexts in which they occur. Chapter IV then traced the basic contour of creedal statements by comparing them with other forms of discourse, locating them first in the context of human language and then in a sharper focus, they were contrasted and compared with other uses of language and finally they were set off from other religious uses of language.

The attention then has been so far focused on the "I believe" part of the creedal statement which has been shown to be performative in the original Austinian sense of doing specific linguistic tasks aside from merely stating. But a creedal statement has also precisely a staing task. The verb "believe" has an object which can be rephrased into a further statement, for example, that "God is Father Almighty." A creedal statement has an "I believe *in*" and "I believe *that*" aspect. The first is its illocutionary aspect and the second, its locutionary aspect. And although a creedal statement as a type of utterance is distinctively illocutionary in character as the previous analyses have shown, its illocutionary forces are linked with its cognitive content which constitutes its locutionary aspect. R.W. Sleeper calls attention to this point:

> In philosophy of religion in the elucidation of believing, this factual element is of the utmost importance. For, though feeling, emotions, hoping, desiring and valuing all have their places in believing-in, they do not exhaust it. ... For the claim of the believer is precisely that there *is* an object of his believe-in. Moreover, it is the claim of the *religious* believer that God is that object, that God is not just an anthropomorphic projection of a moral ideal... And it is the even bolder claim of the Christian that God actually was incarnate in Jesus and not just that the disciples decided that he was.[1]

---

1 R.W. Sleeper, "On Believing" in *Religious Studies*, II, 1 (October, 1966), 92.

In Wittgensteinian terms, the grammar of "believing is linked up with the grammar of the believed in proposition." (OC, 313) It is with this assertive proposition that this reflection on "meaning" will be primarily concerned. First, an attempt will be made to explore the meaning of "meaning" in relation to statements in general and then the meaningfulness of creedal statements will be discussed according to the uses of meaning thus established. This eventually leads the discussion to the question of "truth" regarding creedal statements.

I. *The Different Uses of "Meaning"*

Instead of going into theories of meaning in the exploration of nuances of "meaning" regarding statements, it seems better to glean these nuances from actual examples. Note the various ways in which the word "meaning" and its correlates are used in the following:
1. Does "The algib filtend felresly" have a meaning?
2. "The table blinked its eyes and moaned" is meaningless.
3. Do the statements "She is dead" and "She has gone to her eternal rest" have the same meaning?
4. It is meaningless to say today "The present King of France is wise".
5. The proposition "Cats think, only they are too clever to show it" is meaningless.
6. The saying "Love is as strong as death" has become meaningful to me.

The foregoing list is not exhaustive but illustrative of the different uses of the word "meaning." In the first example, the lack of meaning is due to the combination of made-up words that have no established use in the English language. The second example although it fulfills the condition of usingconventional words combined in a correct grammatical syntax nevertheless lacks meaning, because it makes an invalid prediction of concepts. The word "table" is not used to designate something having eyes or physical organs necessary for moaning. This is usually called a category mistake.[2] It is of course not unthinkable that one with a very fertile imagination could construct a situation where this phrase can have a poetical or some

---

[2] For a detailed treatment of category mistakes, see Gilbert Ryle, *The Concept of Mind*, 92.

kind of meaning. The point is that it has no literal prosaic meaning in the ordinary context. The third example uses "meaning" in a similar way as "information." Thus one can rephrase the question into: "Does the statement 'She is dead' convey the same information as the statement 'She has gone to her eternal rest'?" We are not concerned here as to whether they do give the same information or not. The point is that the use of "meaning" in this example is synonymous to "information." The fourth example shows the reference aspect of "meaning," that there is a use of "meaning" which requires the criterion of reference. Thus in the fourteenth century, such a statement would have been meaningful, because then there was a king of France. The statement now can be used meaningfully in the context of a game or of a trick to find out whether someone is ignorant of there being a king of France or not at present. But it cannot now be used meaningfully as a serious assertion. The fifth example focuses on the use of "meaning" with special regard to factual empirical assertions which necessitates the possibility of verification or falsification as criterion for meaningfulness. The last example illustrates the nuance of "meaning" of statements designating the point, importance or significance of a statement.

In the application of these uses of the word "meaning" to creedal statements, certain preliminary remarks are necessary. It must be repeated that it cannot be the task of this thesis to discuss the meaning of the content of any specific creedal statement. This hermeneutical task belongs to the dogmatic theologian in collaboration with the exegete. Here the task is to investigate the *meaningfulness* of the creedal statement as a type of statement. Secondly, certain uses of "meaning" can be presupposed to be applicable to creedal statements without any difficulty, namely the purely grammatical ones. Creedal statements do use conventionally accepted words and follow the ordinary rules of syntax. The surface grammar of creedal statements do not pose problems which sometimes theological jargon does. They usually are straightforward statements using words belonging to the ordinary spoken language and in the way they are usually made use of. The nuance of "meaning" as "significance" or "importance" is the burden of another chapter. What remains to be discussed here are therefore the following uses:
1. Informative potentiality
2. Referential Aspect
3. Verifiability or Truth Aspect

These uses are not sharply distinct from one another. They overlap and supplement each other in some ways. A categorization, though artificial, is nevertheless indispensible for analysis.

II. *The Informative Potentiality of Creedal Statements*

Informative potentiality as a use of "meaning" of statements requires that the statement appeal to the addressee's faculty of understanding evoking a cognitive response of some sort. That it may evoke other responses as well is not excluded. For example, the statement "Your mother died" will evoke an emotive response, but this implies that the statement has succeeded in its informative function. But "information" as used in this section is not limited to the sharing of knowledge by one who is in a position to know something with one who is not in a position to know what is the case.[3] The reflections of two people over a problem, even if not resulting in the addition of new knowledge in the sense of material content, is considered informative in the sense that their deliberations appeal to the cognitive faculty of understanding.

As applied to creedal statements therefore, the question of "information" is whether creedal statements have some cognitive content which can be communicated that is potentially able to result in some knowledge. Although affective cognitivity and knowledge by acquaintance are as such relevant to the discussion of creedal statements, in this section, "knowledge" is taken to mean descriptive cognition.

Many philosophical discussions have been made on the cognitivity of religious assertions which include creedal statements.[4] Instead of going through these discussions, it seems more profitable to examine for oneself some creedal statements and see whether they have informative potentiality or not. From the Apostles' Creed, the following creedal propositions are taken as samples:

> God is Father Almighty.
> Jesus is the Son of God.
> Jesus Christ is our Lord.
> He is born of the Virgin Mary.
> The body will rise again.
> Sins can be forgiven.
> Christ will judge the living and the dead.

---

[3] W. Christian, *Meaning and Truth in Religion* (New Jersey: Princeton University Press, 1964), 213.

[4] See Chapter I of this work, pp. 22-31.

First of all, it is clear that the above statements are not tautologies such as the statement, "Black cats are black." They are assertions made by predication of properties or relations to subject concepts. Anyone familiar with the English language will get out of these propositions certain information in the sense defined above. Whether he grasps the whole or even the correct meaning of each statement is at this moment beside the point. He might not know what to do with some statements like "The body will rise again" or "He... was conceived by the Holy Spirit," but even the crudest interpretation he gives to the statement is an evidence of the cognitive content of the statements.

Creedal statements, it must be stated from the outset, do not have as distinctive linguistic force or intention, "to give information," as scientific statements or historical reports have. But neither are they mere exclamations such as a cry for help or a cheer. They are assertions and therefore more directly informative than such exclamations which indirectly likewise give information, i.e. that someone is needing help or in a particular context, that a team is winning a game. But these are implied and not expressed by the exclamations. The information of creedal statements is in contrast expressed by the very statements. Some creedal statements express information similar to that offered by historical statements. But the most important and distinctive creedal statements do not offer such a type of information. The information they give is not something that is gathered from observation or from a personal interview. The informative content of these statements take the form of claims or proposals asimed at answering a common question which can be a sustained enquiry,[5] as for example, "What is the meaning of life?"

III. *The Reference Aspect of Creedal Statements*

Statements with informative potentiality can still lack meaning on another count, namely, if they are meant to be serious assertions but the concepts they use lack reference. Thus the example, "The present King of France is wise," when seriously uttered today, is meaningless for lack of a referent. If a creedal statement has indeed a constative aspect besides being the expression of an attitude or of an emotional state or a resolution, a referential aspect and a truth claim belong to the responsibility and

---

5 Cf. William Christian, *Op. Cit.*, 13.

seriousness of such an utterance. This section will tackle the reference aspect.

It is interesting to note that the reference aspect of creedal statements is a theoretical, not a practical problem. Believers in uttering the traditional creeds and the statements they sometimes formulate on certain occasions, do not have difficulty in referring their thoughts to something or other evoked by the concepts in their statements. These concepts may be vague to them, they may not be able to explain them, but there is no problem in their minds about the reality of the referents of the concepts they use. This is understandable, because believers use the statements in existential contexts in which the concern is mainly with life and how it is lived and for this, clear and distinct concepts are not absolutely necessary. It is only reflective enquiry into these concepts which meet with difficulty. I.M. Crombie recognizes this aspect of the question when he writes:

> In trying to fix the reference range of theological statements, I am trying to fix it *for the critic*, that is, for the man who says he cannot see what religious people are talking about and does not believe that there is anything which can be talked about in such a way. It is only to him that one would ever think of answering the question, "What does 'God' stand for?" To the religious man, the natural answer to such a question is "'God' is the name of the Being who is worthy do be adored."[6]

That is not to say that the clarification of concepts is not of importance to religious living. Reflection on religious concepts is necessary for maturity in religious life just as thoughtful living is necessary for maturity in human life as such. Reflection on religious concepts prevents fanaticism, scrupulosity or some other religious aberration. It likewise ensures a consistency in one's religious acts.

1. Reference Proposals for the Concept "God"

The most important concept of creedal statements which offers a problem of reference is "God." Discussion of the reference aspect of creedal statements will be limited to this word, because it is basic to all other concepts used in the creed.

It must be admitted from the outset that the referent for this word is not as simple and easy to point out as that of such words as "chair," "table," "tree," etc. The history of human thought shows how man has wrest-

---

6 I.M. Crombie, "The Possibility of Theological Statements" in Basil Mitchell, *Op. Cit.*, 13.

led with the concept throughout the ages and the result of his endeavor shows a very wide range of referent proposals. William Christian, in his book *Meaning and Truth in Religion*[7] lists at least nine such reference proposals for the word "God." The following is an abridged summary of this list:

1. Qualities — Ex. "Wisdom is the only thing for which the world is well lost. It means a peace and an inner freedom, without which nothing else is needed." (p. 169)

2. Relations — Ex. "Nothing in the world is better that harmony ... This is the supreme good and the source of all other good things. This is indeed the source of that inner peace and freedom you call wisdom" (p. 171)

3. Particular natural entities— Ex. "The sun is the ultimate source of our life. It makes the corn grow. It gives us warmth. Also its brilliance blinds us. It surpasses all other things in power." (p. 172)

4. Particular human individuals or groups— Ex. "... it is the state, a particular social organization, whci is the source of our values. What would be without it? We are born into it and by its laws and by the subtle powerful influence of its life we become what we are. So if we realize the true spiritual source of our being, we will give our devotion to our country. We will live for it and die for it." (p. 173)

5. Nature — Ex. "... O Nature Sovereign of all beings! And ye adorable daughter of Virtue, Reason and Truth! Remain forever our revered protectors. It is to you appertains the homage of the earth. Show us then, O Nature that which man ought to do, in order to obtain happiness which thou makes him desire." (From Holbach's *Système de la Nature*, quoted in p. 178)

6. Mankind — Ex. "... Towards Humanity, who is for us the only true Great Being, we, The conscious element of whom she is composed, shall henceforth direct every aspect of our life, individual or collective. Our thoughts will be devoted to the knowledge of Humanity, our affections to her love, our actions to her service." (From A. Comte's *System of Positive Polity*, quoted in p. 178)

---

[7] Cf. W. Christian, *Op. Cit.*, 169-182. This list of proposals is for our purpose of showing the variety of reference proposals for the word "God", serviceable, but the list as such does not make sharp enough distinctions to warrant the groupings, between qualities and relations, between pure forms and pure Being, for example.

7. Pure Forms - Ex. "... Is that ultimate a power by which by the very compusion of its fiats, creates the distinctions between good and evil? Or is the ultimate rather a value by which all the powers that there may be, small and great, finite and even infinite, may, indeed must be, judged to which these powers whether they conform or fail to conform to its moral demands, are alike subject in principle?" (From Sterling Lamprecht's *Our Religious Tradition*, quoted in p. 180)

8. Pure Being - Ex. "It is the One, and simply by being itself it gives unity and being to all things. The true goal of life is to be one with it." (p. 181)

9. Transcendent Active Being- Ex. "The being who is the source of all things is not a 'pure being'... He is a being who acts. He creates all good things. ... In every situation of life he is so to speak at work. The end of life is to enjoy his work and obey his will. True joy is found in his service." (p. 182)

Within this ninth type of proposal there are those which consider the tanscendent being as a person or persons: "I believe in God the *Father* Almighty." "There are three *Persons* in God."

If the word "God" could be given so many referents, is it not so nebulously used in creedal statements as to render the statements meaningless? This is not a question that can be answered with a mere "yes" or "no". An attempt at an acceptable answer is to be done in stages. First of all, in the creedal statement, the word "God" is already very much limited in its range of reference, because the Christian concept of God would disregard the first eight proposals taken exclusively and would fix the limit of its range of reference to a self-revealing, trans-empirical personal Reality. This, with all its qualifications, is, of course, not yet as definite and precise as the word "tree." No amount of limitation would render the concept so clearly defined. The crucial question is whether a word must have so definitely defined a referent as that of the word "tree" so as to be used in meaningful discourse. When one pays attention to the utterances in human intercourse, one realizes that many statements which no one would ordinarily consider meaningless, make use of words that are not as clear-cut as the word "tree," or "dog". Many concepts have very fuzzy edges. Consider statements with the word "democracy," "justice," "love," "peace," "freedom," "life," etc. One cannot deny that these are some of the most used words in today's world. People would ordinarily consider talk using such words meaningful, and yet who can make a definite delineation of these concepts?

A single common public aspect evident to all regarding words is not required for their meaningful use. Words are not attached to objects like labels as the logical atomists once claimed. The meaning of a word is therefore not limited to one pointable object or idea. A word can be used in various ways to mean various things, but of course in each use the word refers to something definite, even if its total meaning is not absorbed by its referent nor the totality of its referent exhausted by it.

It is clear that the subject of reference of creedal statements involving the word "God" cannot be fixed on a point in the coordinate system of our empirical world. But the reference aspect of meaning need not provide a difficulty in establishing the meaningfulness of creedal statements if three points are kept in mind: (1) that the coordinate system of empirical reality cannot claim to be all of reality, (2) that words can be used meaningfully even if the concepts they express are not clearly and sharply defined in their comprehension and extension, (3) that there is not just one mode of reference, namely that of physical ostention or mental identification.

2. Modes of Reference of Religious Proposals

William Christian discusses at least five ways of referring to the subject of basic religious proposals, namely: ostention, giving examples, assigning regular effects, assigning extraordinary effects, and interpretation.[8]

Ostensive reference which consists in pointing at something or "giving a definite description locating it in relation to something to which we can point" (p. 185) is not particularly suited to theistic statements, because these statements are not talking about an empirical entity. It can, however, be used by some types of creedal statements of a more historical character as for example, "He suffered under Pontius Pilate."

Referring by giving examples are usually used to determine qualities and relations. When talking about wisdom, for example, one can ask: "Give an example of what you mean by wisdom." And the proposer can mention some acquaintance or historical figure to bring out the quality spoken of: "Socrates was a wise man. He had the quality I mean." Likewise when one is asked, "What do you mean when you say God is almighty?" One can answer, "He brought the Israelites out of Egyptian bondage." A revised version of

---

8 *Ibid.*, 185-192.

this type of referral is used in the so-called negative theology. First the theologian gives examples of things that have the qualities of beauty, goodness, etc. Then he points out the imperfections of these examples so as to suggest something that has no such imperfections - to the perfectly Good and the perfectly Beautiful, to which he gives the name, "God."

Another possibility of referring is by calling attention to some regularity in the course of events and then mentioning the logical subject as the cause of the series. This type of referral is made use of by the classical cosmological argument.

Assigning extraordinary effects goes something like this:

> We introduce some entity M into discourse by mentioning some extraordinary event and saying that M produced it. Instead of some regularity or other in the course of events, we mention an event... marked out in some way from the ordinary course of events and is thus extraordinary. And we say for example, "M is the inventor of the flying machine." (p. 191)

This is the type of referral used in the Old Testament when it identifies Jahwe as the God of the Exodus, a great event in the history of Israel. "I am the Lord thy God who has brought thee out of the Land of Egypt, out of the house of bondage." (Exod. 20, 2)

The fifth mode of reference is by interpretation. Christian describes it thus: "References are made to a whole of which a fact is a part, or to a reality of which a fact is an appearance or manifestations, or to a substance of which a fact is an attribute or an accidental property or to a pure form which particular things approximate." (p. 193) In this mode of reference, the goal of reference must be of another ontological order than the factual starting point. Theistic talk makes use of such a referral when it talks of the world or events as part of a bigger pattern of order, of meaning, of beauty or of perfection.

Again, the above discussed modes of reference cannot claim to exhaust all possible ways of referral. They are treated here to show that there are varieties of reference possibilities which can help in the understanding of what is being talked about. Theistic talk need not exhaust all possible modes of reference before it can be considered meaningful. It is enough that it can answer some of the questions of reference like, "What does this logical subject do?" "What are its effects?" "Is it related in some way to experience? If so, how?" "If it is beyond my experience, in what way is it beyond my experience?" In making use of the above mentioned mode of referrals, theistic talk does give answers to these questions.

IV. *The Truth Aspect of Creedal Statements*

Granting that creedal statements are meaningful according to the reference aspect of meaning, their intention of being serious assertions still require a further aspect of meaning. A statement having a fictive subject, even if it has a referent, is meaningless as a serious assertion, although it can be meaningful in the context of a narrative fiction. For example: "Alice, after her visit to Wonderland, married a prosperous businessman and lived in London for the rest of her life." Creedal statements, if they are serious assertions, must make a truth claim. The question of the possibility of truth or falsehood regarding creedal statements is necessary for the felicity of its informative and referential aspects. W. Christian's sharp delineation of the question deserves to be quoted at length:

> Indeed, whenever a confession declares some referential attitude ... it is fair to hold the speaker responsible for some implicit proposal for belief. If referential attitudes are confessed, proposals for belief are implied. For these attitudes (unlike moods) have objects and a conscious relation to some object, involves some belief about it...
> So if someone utters a confession and does not wish to be held responsible for some belief but wishes, instead to disavow any claim to truth, he ought to make it clear that he is not declaring any referential attitude but only a mood or emotional state...
> In consequence when a referential attitude is declared it is not enough to appraise the confession by using terms which apply directly (a) to the speaker himself, like "naive," "frank," "insincere," and so on (b) to our own reactions as when we say a confession is "embarassing," or "welcome," or (c) to the circumstances in which it is made, as when we say, it is "damaging" or "finicky" and it is not enough to appraise the confession itself... as "interesting," "irrelevant," "trivial," and so on. When a confession conveys an implicit proposal for belief, then we ought to judge what is implicitly proposed.[9]

In short: the confessional statement must be able to undergo the query whether it is saying something which is true or untrue.

In discussing the truth aspect of creedal statements, some preliminary remarks are called for. First, it must be clear that it is not the question here whether creedal statements contain this or that truth claim and whether this or that claim is true or not. The question is merely whether creedal statements are making truth claims or not and what type of truth claims

---

9 W. Christian, *Op. Cit.*, 134 f.

they are making. Furthermore, it is important to realize that even within the traditional creeds, there is a variety of creedal statements and therefore a single paradigm for establishing truth claims will not suffice. It is thus necessary to go over the different ways of establishing truth claims and find out whether one or the other type of creedal statement claims to be true in such a way or not.

1. The Varied Uses of "Truth"

The preceding reflection on reference has shown that creedal statements are not tautologies. These statements do not therefore claim to be logically true such as axiomatic principles of logic and mathematics are. The only other type of truth claim besides logical truth which the logical positivists acknowledged was the empirical truth claim. The present state of discussion on this point seems to have come so far as to despense us from a detailed treatment of the logical positivistic theory of verification and all its subsequent corollaries and substitutes in relation to creedal statements, because it has been subsequently shown to have unjustifiably limited the concepts "verification" and "meaning" to empirical verification and scientific or logical meaning. It is therefore inadequate to account for the meaningfulness of statements of at least partly non-empirical character which creedal statements are. As E.L. Evans aptly puts it:

> To say of a given sentence that it can be verified is not to say anything about the meaningfulness of the sentence, but to characterize it as being a sentence of a certain type, an empirical sentence. If we cannot apply the verification principle to a sentence, such a sentence cannot be an empirical one. The question of whether it is meaningful is a further question, quite independent of the question whether it is empirical or not.[10]

The creeds have statements with a historical content and which makes some historical factual claims (i.e. the articles on Christ being born of Mary, having suffered under Pontius Pilate, etc.) Such statements clearly involve truth conditions in which empirical facts are relevant. In such statements, the historical facts of the case comprise the necessary, though not the sufficient, conditions of their being true. If there never was such a person as Jesus Christ, the Christian claim that Jesus is the Saviour of Mankind is assuredly false. These historical assertions fall under the

---

10 E.L. Evans, "On Meaning and Verification," in *Mind*, 63 (1953) 16 f.

scrutiny of historical methods for the establishment of their truth or falsity. It must however be noted here that even these statements with historical content are making more than just factual historical claims and these supra-historical assertions are beyond the competence of the historical critical method to judge. If then creedal statements are neither tautologies nor pure empirical claims, and if they are not reducible to mere historical claims, in what sense are they claims, and in what sense can they be considered true or false?

In venturing to answer these questions, some factors form a starting point, namely: (1) the varied uses of the word "true," (2) the fact of the variety of uses of creedal statements, and (3) the notion of grammatical claims. The first two have been discussed. There remains the third factor to be explained.

2. The Notion of "Grammatical Claims"

Stuart Brown in his book, *Do Religious Claims Make Sense?*[11] offers a wider and more detailed treatment of the notion of "grammatical claims" which he coins on the basis of some Wittgensteinian insights into language. It will be discussed here only in so far as it helps in the development of the present discussion.

Grammar, according to Wittgenstein "tells us what kind of object anything is." (PI, 373) Whether a sentence made a sense or not depended on whether it was constructed according to the rules of grammar. Furthermore, there are propositions which state what makes and what does not make sense to say in a specific grammatical system. Wittgenstein calls these "illustrated turns of speech." (PI, 295) These may either be forthright propositions on grammar as exemplified by grammar rules. (For example, in the Spanish language, the stressed adjectival forms of the pronoun comes always after the principal word and agrees with it in number and gender.) They may also be veiled grammatical propositions as for example the statement, "You can't count through the whole series of cardinal numbers," (BB, 54) These propositions are not making matter-of-fact claims as their surface grammar may lead one to think. In the second example, for instance, nothing is being claimed about human power or about the quantity of car-

---

[11] Cf. Stuart Brown, *Do Religious Claims Make Sense?* (London: SCM Press, Ltd., 1969), 104 ff.

dinal numbers. It merely points to the use of the words "cardinal numbers" in language, that it is used as a logical concept with a non-empirical referent about which it would make no sense to say that one can stop counting it, as one would a basket of apples. Grammatical propositions of this kind are "true" in the sense that their use corresponds to the usage in a given linguistic system. They are not experiential claims, and they are not true in the sense of empirical truth. This reflection is necessary in the discussion of the question of truth of creedal statements. A review of the various uses of creedal statements is likewise necessary.

It has been established in the previous chapters that there are various ways of using creedal statements. There is the public official use of creedal statements expressed mainly in the traditional formulae usually in a liturgical context. There is the use of the creedal formula as doctrinal norm or as a summary of the belief of the community. There is the theological-philosophical context where creedal formulae are objects of reflection. There are the private acts of faith with less rigid formulations based on one or the other article of the creeds, uttered usually in limiting situations or when one is challenged about what one believes.

Granting the indisputable givenness (Vorhandensein) of Christian religious discourse, we venture to make the following affirmations:

1. Creedal statements in their use as doctrinal norms and summary of the belief of the community state the basic presuppositions of the Christian way of life and mode of discourse. As such they function in some way like veiled grammatical claims and are therefore true in the sense that grammatical claims are true. Within the context of the Christian way of life, they form the linguistic framework within which the meaningfulness, the truth or falsity of other statements in the Christian religious discourse are to be judged. As Stuart Brown puts it: "Any religion in so far as it purports to embody a distinctive conception of reality must embody what I have called 'grammatical claims' or what would in Christian terminology be called 'articles of faith.'"[12] Their meaning and truth as grammatical claims depend on their adequacy in articulating the Christian experience and way of life and on their inner coherence and consistency.

2. The other uses of creedal statements as public testimony to a com-

---

12 *Ibid.*, 147.

munity of faith, as doxological acclamations in worship, private expressions of confidence and trust, etc., in as much as they are a Christian religious use of language are to be judged in their content as meaningful or meaningless, true or false (in the sense of genuine or superstitious) according to the linguistic framework thus provided by the articles of the faith.

3. Speculative use of creedal statements in theological and philosophical discussions are meaningful or meaningless, true or false (in the sense of faithful or unfaithful to the Christian conception of reality) according to their inner coherence and in correspondence to the grammatical propositions of Christian religious discourse.

The first affirmation, being the most important of the three assertions stated above, needs a more detailed discussion:

3. The Grammatical Function of Creedal Statements

First of all, to understand what it means for creedal statements to be grammatical claims, of Christian religious discourse, it is necessary to be aware that both language in general and Christian religious discourse in particular have non-linguistic presuppositions which form their bedrock. These presuppositions have to do with how the world and human life is, in the case of language in general and with a conception and experience of reality in the case of Christian religious discourse. The consideration of this non-linguistic bedrock of language is the main concern of Wittgenstein's last notes, *On Certainty*. The scope of this work does not allow a detailed treatment of this matter. It suffices to mention some points relevant to the present concern. Since these notes were an elaboration of the concept of language games already discussed in *Philosophical Investigations* an important consideration will first be mentioned, namely that language games are embedded in forms of life. Dilman sums up Wittgenstein's position thus:

> Language games are based on the participants' matter of course actions and reactions to certain situations and on the agreement in these reactions... The actions and reactions in the weave of which verbal expressions are used and transitions made from one expression to another as when we make an inference, are part of the language game. (PI, 7) Apart from them, there could be no consistent practice with words, no connection between language and reality - in short no language. They are an important part of the framework which provided the posts where our words are stationed; they determine the grammar of our words.[13]

---

13 Ilham Dilman "On Wittgenstein's Last Notes: *On Certainty*: (1950-51)" in *Philosophy*, 176 (April, 1971), 166.

These non-linguistic presuppositions, being the conditions for the possibility of language, are not open to question. This is an important claim of *On Certainty*: "A language game is only possible if one trusts something." (OC, 509) Trust, belief and conviction lie at the foundations of speech, reasoning and judgement and are presupposed in the business of living: "My life shows that I know or am certain that there is a chair over there, or a door and so on. I tell a friend, e.g. 'Take that chair over there,' 'Shut the door,' etc. etc." (OC, 7) Agreement in forms of life which underlies the possibility of speech and communication involves agreement in beliefs. (OC, 56; PI, 241-242) These beliefs in which there is common agreement are held together and constitute a system: "When we first begin to believe anything, what we believe is not a single proposition, it's a whole system of propositions. (Light dawns gradually over the whole)." (OC, 41; Cf. OC, 211) This system of propositions gives a whole picture. (OC, 92, 209) These beliefs are acquired by instruction:

> The child learns to believe a host of things. I.e. it learns to act according to beliefs. Bit by bit there forms a system of what is believed, and in that system some things stand unshakeably fast and some are more or less liable to shift. What stands fast does so, not because it is intrinsically obvious or convincing, it is rather held fast by what lies around it. (OC, 144; Cf. OC, 159-161)

These beliefs constitute a common understanding that binds people together and in them we have a measure of what is possible, intelligible and reasonable.

Wittgenstein discusses at length such a non-linguistic presupposition which might not be the best example but is the only one that was readily available. In OC, 1 ff., he discusses the reliability of the senses as one such presupposition which lies at the bedrock of language. There is no point in questioning one's senses, because it can neither be proved or disproved. To try to justify it is like trying to lift oneself by one's bootstraps. If one has to talk in a human way, one must take this for granted.

This lengthy discussion of the non-linguistic presuppositions of language is necessary to see how things are with the presuppositions of the language game of Christian religious discourse. The grammatical claims (articles of faith) of this discourse are likewise based on non-linguistic presuppositions that condition its possibility. To be very cautious, we mention two minimum presuppositions, namely, the theistic presupposition which conditions the possibility of the discourse being religious, and the presuppositions implied in the main articles of faith about Christ, as a condition for its being a *Christian* religious discourse. The reality of God and the claim that Christ is God incarnate cannot be proved in any way satisfactory to the human mind. Neither can they be disproved. No human instrument can validate or invalidate them in the same way that one can validate or invalidate empirical claims. But they are the conditions which must be presupposed if one decides to engage in the Christian religious discourse. They are its starting point, its "proto-phenomena."

The analogy between Christian creedal discourse and language in general has of course its limits. The presuppositions of human language are not to be questioned, because there is no alternative to human language. But can this be said of Christian religious discourse? This question will be treated after the possibilities offered by the analogy has been exhausted.

It is necessary to go back to the point where the analogy still serves a purpose. The rules of the grammar of language in general change, because as Wittgenstein puts it, "the riverbed of thoughts may change." (OC, 97) Vocabularies grow, syntactical conditions evolve, the meanings of words change. Applying this to changes in regard to the grammatical claims of Christian religious discourse brings out some questions to the theologian, the "grammarian" of the Christian religious discourse. Can there be no changes in creedal statements according to the progress of human experience, of human self-understanding, and of his understanding of the phenomenon he considers divine? Which creedal statements can suffer such changes and which cannot undergo such changes without putting an end to the discourse as such? This brings the discussion to the question of the rank or value of the creedal statements as grammatical claims.

The grammar rules in a language have varying weights in deciding the intelligibility of a sentence, depending upon the milieu of a specific linguistic system. the rules of punctuation, for example, may be less important in English as they are in German. Within the same system, i.e. in the English language, rules of punctuation are less important than the rules of agreement of subject and predicates. Similarly, the articles of the creed have varying degrees of importance. The article on the communion of saints or about the descent into hell are less important than the articles on God and the redeeming acts of Christ. A statement can disregard certain grammar rules and remain meaningful. But there is a minimum of grammatical conditions which have to be observed for the statement to be intelligible. A parallel question may be posed to the theologian as to which articles of the faith form the minimum conditions for the possibility of meaningful Christian religious discourse. An effort in answering this question could perhaps cut out on inconsequential theological discussions and controversial verbiage and maintain a healthy and refreshing pluralism in such discussions.

The question of meaningfulness of creedal statements has been discussed as a question internal to the Christian religious discourse. It has been asserted that creedal statements used in private and speculative contexts are meaningful and are judged "true" or "false" within Christian discourse in which creedal statements as "articles of faith" perform a grammatical function. These are meaningful as grammatical claims and are true in a similar sense as grammatical truth in a linguistic system. These creedal grammatical truths however are true only in correspondence to the non-linguistic factors which they presuppose which have limited to the ontological reality of God and the historical reality and significance of Christ. This leads the discussion back to the question left open earlier. The question was whether these presuppositions could reamain unquestioned as has to be done in the case of the presuppositions of language in general. Though both the presuppositions of language in general and at least the most basic presupposition (i.e. the theistic presupposition) in Christian religious discourse cannot be proved, nevertheless unlike the presuppositions of language, those of Christian religious discourse are open to question, because there are alternatives to Christian religious discourse. When one is born as a human being, one must speak human language, but being born human does not oblige one to speak the Christian religious discourse.

There is thus an external aspect to the question of meaning regarding creedal statements. In this aspect, the meaning of creedal statements is tied up with that of the whole system of Christian religious discourse and with its non-linguistic presuppositions. Even if there is no question of proof, there is at least the question of justification. Implied in the profession of faith is a form of life. If this form of life is meaningful in the sense of being significant and true in the sense of being relevant to human experience, it guarantees the meaning and truth of creedal statements which base themselves on it. The question may be formulated thus: "Why does it make sense to speak in a Christian religious way?" which is a linguistic phrasing corresponding to the question, "Why does the Christian belief make sense?" The next chapter will discuss this question.

Chapter VI

THE "FORM OF LIFE" OF CREEDAL STATEMENTS

Chapter III and IV attempted to trace the contours of the linguistic activity of confessing one's belief as a religious activity. This activity was shown to be constituted by varying forms of speech acts which have overlapping characteristics as well as differing nuances - from the simple and more spontaneous acclamations to the more conventionalized recitation of the creed in the context of worship which still had the nuance of acclamations. Further investigation of the creed disclosed a pledge character in the baptismal creedal profession which reached an intensity in the confessional utterance of the martyrs during their trial which took on a witness character. In the synodal creed, the commissive aspect receded and the creed acquired a more didactic, normative character.

To understand these various linguistic activities, it is not enough to get a sample of a creedal statement and examine it isolated from the stream of life in which it is formed. This is the kind of error which has given rise to the interminable philosophical and theological discussions about the "existence of God." When one forgets that this phrase has its *Sitz im Leben* in a religious (creedal) context, then one gets into all sorts of problems (i.e. verifiability, problem of proof, etc.) which could have been avoided if the phrase were not taken as though it came from scientific, logical or philosophical context, but were located in its religious setting.

It is therefore inevitable that an investigation of creedal statements should entail an investigation of its form of life. Christian creedal statements are woven into a network of human activities. It is intertwined with the linguistic and non-linguistic activities of the Christian way of life. It is, of course, impossible to discuss all the factors and activities that enter into the Christian way of life. The interest here will only be on those which will throw light on the linguistic act under study. The task of this chapter will be:

1) to characterize the Christian way of life by investigating its primary presuppositions.
2) to investigate the main factors in this way of life which account for its *creedal* way of articulation.
3) to point out in a general way the rationale of the Christian way of life thus showing the sense (significance) of Christian religious discourse and thus also of its basic statements - the creedal statements.

The reflections in the following two sections will sound more theological than linguistic, but this is inevitable, because in explaining the Christian way of life, one has to use its language. However, these reflections differ from theological treatises in that they are merely descriptive and not evaluative or prescriptive as theology often is.

I. *The Primary Presuppositions of the Christian Way of Life*

The Christian way of life, as has been pointed out earlier in Chapter V, has two kinds of presuppositions, meta-physical and historical presuppositions. A discussion of these presuppositions aims to explain at least in part, the distinctive and non-negotiable content of the Christian creed which will in turn account for the creedal nature of the Christian religious discourse.

1. The Theistic Presupposition

The meta-physical presupposition of the Christian way of life consists in a *theistic view* of the world. Karl Rahner, a Christian (Catholic) theologian articulates this world view thus:

> The objective ultimate ground of all reality which is present only by precisely *not* being a part of our world-image and which is the endgoal of our movement to acquire a view of the world, a goal essentially beyond the reach of our own power, we call God.[1]

This world-view thus posits a personal Reality who created the world, on which the meaning of this created world is anchored. But the theistic world-view does not only see this Reality called God as standing at the "beginning" of the world, i.e. as Creator, but likewise at its "consummation." The Christian theistic world view has thus an eschatological orien-

---
1 Karl Rahner, "Science as a 'Confession'?", 388.

tation. The Christian does not only look at the world as having a meaning outside of itself (ontological transcendence), he also posits a temporal transcendence. He sees the world as moving into its fullness of meaning in the "new heaven and the new earth."

2. The Christological Presupposition

The historical presupposition is not a separate assumption, but is related to the first presupposition. For it consists in the belief that this transcendent personal Reality called God, who created the world, has intervened in human history by revealing himself to man. This process of revelation, so the Christian claims, reached its climax in Jesus of Nazareth, who is God incarnate. It is *not* the historical reality of Jesus of Nazareth, which constitutes this second presupposition, but the *significance* attributed to him - that he is the fullness of the revelation of God of himself, and that the message he brought to the world is the message of salvation for the whole of mankind. This entails, of course, other presuppositions about sin, grace, and so on, but the discussion will limit itself to those which directly affect the main concern of this thesis, which is to understand creedal statements.

How do these basic presuppositions affect creedal statements? They do so mainly in the content and structure of the creed. The creedal formulae, even when differing in terminology, or even in the number of articles they express, are structurally built on these presuppositions: God, Christ, salvation. In its contents, the Christian creedal discourse is first and foremost God-talk. There are many elements in Christian religious discourse which are in common with other forms of discourse, which it can dispense with, without ceasing to be itself. The theistic discourse is likewise shared by other forms of discourse, but it is something that the Christian religious discourse cannot abandon without ceasing to be itself. If indeed as Paul van Buren has announced, the word "God" is dead[2], then Christian religious discourse would likewise be dead. John Macquarrie sees the point quite clearly:

---

2 Cf. Paul van Buren, *Secular Meaning of the Gospel* (London: The Macmillan Co., 1963). In this work, P. van Buren reduces religious propositions to historical and ethical statements.

> I have asserted quite bluntly that theology cannot fail to talk
> of God. Perhaps there are some Christian doctrines so perpheral
> that we could, if necessary, get along without them. There are
> probably very few such doctrines, for the Christian faith has de-
> veloped a unity, and even doctrines that seem peripheral may make
> their contribution to the understanding of the whole. Yet supposing
> we were to allow that some doctrine might dispensible, we would
> never reckon the doctrine of God among them. This doctrine has a
> central place and is presupposed in all others.[3]

More succinctly and forcefully, in a more linguistic formulation, Ogden drives home the same point: "However absurd talking about God might be, it could never be so obviously absurd as talking of the Christian faith without God."[4] It is only in the context of theistic talk that Christian religious discourse talks about Christ and his way of salvation. The demise of the "God is dead" theology and its lack of success in preaching an atheistic Christianity show the basic role of the theistic presupposition in the Christian religious discourse. Without it, talk on Christ and his way of salvation may, of course, take place, but then it would altogether be a new language game.

II. *Factors that Condition Creedal Statements*

The preceding section has tackled the task of accounting for the "Christian-ness" of Christian creedal discourse. The following paragraphs will attempt to account for its being *creedal*. But first it is necessary to show that Christian religious discourse is indeed basically creedal. In the comparison of creedal statements with other linguistic activities in Christian religious discourse, one saw how difficult it was to obtain a sharp focus. There were no clear boundaries which separated creedal statements from other religious speech acts. Not only that, the creed appeared to permeate all these; it provided the subject matter for these forms of discourse and in some cases it conditioned the felicity of these other discourses as speech acts. Prayer, for example, is ultimately based on the creedal assertion that God is a loving Father. In fact, in some cases, the creeds are used as prayers. Proclamation in its various forms (catechizing,

---

[3] J. Macquarrie, *God and Secularity* (London: Lutterworth Press, 1968), 14.

[4] Schubert Ogden, *The Reality of God* (London: SCM Press, Ltd., 1967), 14.

preaching, and so forth) presuppose that those engaging in it believe what they are saying and their activities can even indeed be interpreted as indirect confessional acts. But indirect confession of beliefs has a sense only if there is a direct confession of belief. Theological talk would have no object of reflection if there were no creedal statements. The point of this review is to emphasize the fact that Christian religious discourse is primarily *creedal* in character.

1. The Faith-Character of the Christian Way of Life

The question now is: "What is it in the Christian way of life which gives rise to this *creedal* characterization of its articulation?" Reflection on the Christian way of life shows that it is primarily a "faith activity." The starting point of this way of life, as shown in the preceding section, is *revelation* and not investigation, speculation or experimentation. Therefore that which confronts the Christian is not empirical evidence or logical insight but a *testimony*. René Latourelle writes:

> Christian revelation is a very specific reality. It is not the result of man's speculation about God but is rather an effect stemming from an initiative on the part of the living God who leaves the realm of the mysterious and intervenes in our history. Revelation is not *gnosis* but testimony and the testimony of those who are the mouth of Yahweh (the prophets) and the testimony of the Son who assumes a language and man's body to express to men the love of a Father.[5]

When man is confronted by evidence either through investigation or experiments, he is moved to intellectual conviction. When he is confronted with a logical argument his reaction is cognitive insight. What happens when he is confronted by testimony? His response can only be either belief or unbelief. The Christian response to the testimony he encounters in revelation is the many-faceted human response called *faith*. This testimonial aspect of faith is translated into layman's language by Oraison thus:

> It occured to me that it might be a good idea to express the reality of faith somewhat whimsically by saying, "I am the man who saw the man who saw the bear." That is not as irreverent as it sounds, because the essence of it is from St. Paul. It is what was called

---

[5] R. Latourelle, "Revelation, History and Incarnation" in *The Word: Readings in Theology*, compiled at the Canisianum (Innsbruck: P.J. Kenedy and Sons, 1964), 27.

> *fides ex auditu* - "faith by hearsay" when theologians insisted on expressing themselves in Latin. And it all began when Andrew, the brother of Simon Peter met Peter on the day after *the* encounter and said to him, "We found the Messiah, that is, the Christ."[6]

Countless books have been written attempting to understand and analyse the phenomenon of faith. Here it is sufficient to point out some of its aspects which are mirrored in the activity of confessional statements which is its linguistic expression.

Juan Alfaro summarizes the characteristics of faith thus:

> Modern exegetes are agreed that faith includes knowledge of a saving event, confidence in the word of God, man's humble submission and personal self-surrender to God, fellowship in life with Christ and a desire for perfect union with him beyond the grave: faith is man's comprehensive "Yes" to God revealing himself as man's saviour in Christ.[7]

If faith is the main response of the Christian to the testimony which confronts him, it is no wonder that in the development of this response into a way of life, the main activity would be "faith activity." This is of course expressed in many ways, linguistic and non-linguistic. In its linguistic expression, this response is articulated directly in what has been made the subject matter of this investigation - in the creedal statements. In studying the forces of this linguistic activity, we have detected the same constative, behabitive, commissive aspects which have corresponding aspects in faith.

2. The Social Aspect of the Christian Way of Life

Another factor in the Christian way of life which conditions the creedal aspect of Christian religious discourse is its *communal aspect*. The experience of the revelation is not an individual experience like, for example, the mystical experience. It demands surely a very high degree of individual commitment, but this in the context of a community of faith, in the *ecclesia*. Ecclesial unity called after John and Paul, the *koinonia* is one of the earliest and deepest concern of those who found themselves sharing the same faith.[8]

---

6 Marc Oraison, *Strange Voyage: The Autobiography of a Non-Conformist* (Garden City: Doubleday and Co., Inc., 1970), 14.

7 Juan Alfaro, "Faith" in *Sacramentum Mundi*, 1968 ed., vol. II, 213 f.

8 Piet Fransen, "Unity and Confessional Statements," unpublished manuscript, 5.

The Christian way of life, being a human social phenomenon, follows socialogical laws. There is a sense in which human beings "construct reality" in which they live. They usually start doing things unreflectively, of course, with some immediate intention. In the process of community building there appears very soon a *process of legitimation* to ensure personal security and the coherence of the group.[9] By legitimation Berger means "socially objectivated knowledge that serves to explain and justify the social order."[10] This is also often termed *rationalization*. It provides answers to questions about the reason for institutional arrangements. At first these legitimations are not integrated. Later on, they are organized into a larger interpretative system by which the varying partial legitimations are integrated into a greater whole which Berger terms "a symbolic universe."[11] According to this process of legitimation, society is the outcome of many and varying legitimation processes of men belonging to the same group. This integrated and systematized interpretation of the social univers exercises a great influence upon the people who have been constructing it. It becomes in social terms "an objective reality, independent as such from the individuals who are continuously confronted with it."[12] It is assimilated by the individuals of the group in a *process of internalisation*. There is thus created a reciprocal movement from the individuals towards further construction of reality and from the created society to the individuals. This results in a greater cohesion of the community. The members tend to think the same truths and to act in unity. They acquire common patterns of behaviour.

The Christian community, the *ecclesia* also went through the same sociological process explained in the preceding paragraphs. The Church, too, started unreflectively to live according to the way of life Christ taught his disciples. In a slow process, she "constructed" different forms of legitimations - taken from the Old Testament, the doctrines of Christ, the traditions of the local churches and from the different activities of the Church - kerygmatic, catechetical, liturgical, missionary and even polemical. The differences in the Gospels of the four evangelists, the variety in liturgy

---

9 Cf. Peter Berger, *The Sacred Canopy: Element of a Sociological Theory of Religion* (Garden City: Doubleday and Co., Inc., 1969), 29 ff.

10 *Ibid.*, 30.

11 Berger, cited in Fransen, *Op. Cit.*, 4.

12 *Loc. Cit.*

and the plurality of confessions of faith and in the structure of the communities point to the existence of this process of legitimation in the early Church.[13] These various legitimations were then directed to the consolidation of the Church - towards the deepening of the unity of the members among themselves and with Christ. One manifestation of this growth in unity was the emergence of a "Christian language", in the context of which the impulse towards confessional statements is to be located. Piet Fransen points out this connection as follows:

> If it is true that the deepest heart of Christianity is God's active and loving presence to everybody of us and to us all together, then it is also true that on the existential level, this deepest unity of the Church has to realize itself in a common language and in a common way of life.[14] That is what we see happening in the Early Church, the slow birth of a common Christian language, at the same time the result and fruit of her deeper unity and the human source of her real communion in faith. Because we are attracted to God by one faith, we look for one language and this one language directs, defends and maintains our unity in faith.
> In this light we understand why confessions of faith originated almost spontaneously in the Church from its very beginning.[15]

This discussion of the social factor of the Christian way of life shows not only the impulse that gave rise to creedal statements, but likewise the specific social character of the creed in its pledge and symbola forms which presuppose a community of faith.

3. The Missionary Factor

The Christian way of life includes necessarily a missionary activity. The Conciliar document on the Missions, *Ad Gentes* states categorically: "The pilgrim Church is missionary by her very nature." (AG, I, 2) The presupposition that the revelatory message was primarily a salvific message explains the Church's claim at universality - in the horizontal and vertical sense. In other words, it claims that this salvific message is for all men and for all times. In its *horizontal* dimension, missionary activity consists in proclaiming this message by word and testifying to it by life. Missionary proclamation finds its substance (contents) and its igniting

---

13 Fransen, *Op. Cit.*, 5.

14 Piet Fransen's use of the terms "common language" and "common way of life" is not expressedly Wittgensteinian, but resembles Wittgenstein's use of "language game" and "form of life".

15 Fransen, *Op. Cit.*, 7.

point in the creedal statements. It proclaims to those who are not yet
members of the community of faith what this community believes, confesses
to and teaches to its own members. In its direct and conscious "converting"
intention, it is a development and intensification of that zeal and self-
commitment which is present in an implicit manner in the confessional utterance. By confessing one's belief, one indirectly expresses that this
belief is of value to oneself and therefore also a possible value for others.
But the confessional utterance is not yet a positive invitation to non-
members to join the community of faith. Missionary provlamation is such
an explicit invitation.

In its *vertical* dimension, the universal aspect in the Christian way
of life involves the *traditional* aspect of faith. If the Christian message
of salvation is for all times, there is a need of handing over from one
generation to the other "spiritual experience of the Church throughout
history as cumulatively expressed in her language, her doctrine and her
way of life, what we were used to call tradition."[16] Every concrete act
of faith of each generation presupposes this what J.B. Metz calls the
"memoria Christi."[17] which is here taken simply to mean tradition as explained above. The confessional statements are the public and condensed
articulation, the "Erinnerungsformeln"[18] of this "memoria."

The missionary activity of the Christian way of life thus accounts for
the witness (commissive) character of the creed as well as its traditional,
conservative (constative) function.

4. The Liturgical Aspect

The idea of the "memoria" brings the discussion to another activity
of the Christian way of life, namely, its cultic activity. The "memoria"
is not only preserved by its being handed down through preaching, but by
its being handed down through its re-enactment in the liturgical celebra-
tion of the Christian community. In fact the word "memoria" is originally
located in this context and is to be traced back to the words of Christ
"Do this in commemoration of me" (Lk. 22, 19) referring to the first

---

16 *Ibid.*, 26.

17 Cf. Metz, et.al., *Diskussion zur "politischen Theologie"*, Mainz-München, 1969, 267-301, esp. 284-291.

18 *Ibid.*, 289.

eucharistic meal.

Again the cultic activity consists, not only of ceremonies, symbols and gestures, but likewise of words. It has a linguistic aspect. And since the main drama enacted in the liturgy is the dialogical exchange between God's self-relevation and man's faith response, it is not surprising that the creed, the linguistic crystallization of this response, should be made use of. As has been elsewhere pointed out,[19] the early Church used the brief creedal acclamations in its worship and the three traditional creeds have been used in the liturgy of the Church throughout its history. The doxological (behavitive) character of the creed is thus to be located in the cultic activity of the Christian way of life.

To summarize: The basically *creedal* character of the Christian religious discourse is accounted for by the kind of activities found in the Christian way of life - communal witnessing, proclaiming, worshipping - all of which flow, in one way or the other, from its "faith-activity."

To round up the discussion of a form of life such as the Christian way of life, and therefore of the discussion of Christian religious discourse, which is its articulation, it is important to tackle the question of its credentials. Of course, it is to be recognized that its most obvious credential is its being given (Vorhandensein) in linguistic terms, in the fact that Christian religious discourse is being spoken. But just as it is legitimate to ask of anything, why it is, so is the question why the Christian way of life or form of discourse is. This question is, in fact, quite necessary with regard to this discourse, because of its specifically creedal aspect. One gives evidences together with empirical assertions, one demonstrates logical arguments, but one offers some credentials for belief, or as the ordinary usage puts it, one "justifies" one's beliefs. In other words, justification belongs to the grammar of belief. This is *not* to say that one must discover or invent *a-priori* reasons for Christian religious discourse, but being confronted with the fact that it is, one asks what in it justifies its being spoken. This question will be tackled by the last two sections of this thesis.

---

[19] See Chapter III, p. 63 of this thesis.

III. *Internal Justification of Christian Religious Discourse*

This first part will survey the reasons Christians themselves give for their creedal utterances. It will therefore see the question from within the system of Christian discourse.

It has been shown in the previous chapter that creedal statements are meant to be serious assertions and affirmations. To make such serious assertions implies that one is ready to give good reasons for uttering them. As Mats Furberg, paraphrasing Austin's view of speech acts, writes: "A serious utterance does in our world entitle the audience to infer that the speaker thinks that he, when asked to, can back it up in a way appropriate to it."[20]

In the case of Christian belief, that which is asserted is not even ordinarily easy to discern. Christian belief utterances are not so much inevitable affirmations of clear perception but are more decisional utterances which makes "backing up" doubly necessary. For the same reason, they lend themselves to being challenged as the history of Christianity shows. This accounts for the development of a systematic justification of Christian creedal statements in the Church which can be traced as far back as the time of the apostles. We read in 1 Peter 13, 15: "... always have your answer ready for people who ask you the reason for the hope that you all have, but give it with courtesy, respect and with clear conscience."

The following paragraphs will select examples of justification done by believers in different contexts. There is no pretense at categorization, but there will be an attempt to get varying examples so as to disclose as many kinds of reasons given as possible.

There is, first of all, the case of a convert who is making up his mind to be baptized. He can reflect upon and see sense in the Christian affirmation about love that goes beyond the conventional forms and includes enemies in its embrace. He can see it as the solution for the physical survival of mankind engaged in an egoistic rat race. He might discern in Christ's audacious claims (i.e. "I am the Way, the Truth and the Life"; "He who does not believe in me shall be condemned"; "I have overcome the world," and so on) the only explanation of Christ's impact on men of all times. For him, it would otherwise be unexplainable how a young man in his

---

20 Mats Furberg, *Saying and Meaning*, 91.

thirties, who lived in a relatively obscure life who left no written records of himself, who was executed as a political prisoner, could have had such a life and death impact on people of different races, stations in life, culture and temperaments, if he had not been what he claimed to be. The convert may furthermore see the justice of the punishment of sin, the possibility of forgivenesss, the probability to hope for an eternal life. He might also, of course, realize that certain belief utterances have in themselves no sense until one views them under a creedal presupposition which, in itself, makes sense. Finally, he might see that aside from the possibility of seeing a meaning in each of the belief utterances and the seeing of the meaninglessness of others, that the Christian way of life as a whole gives a sense of direction of his life. This brings in the kinds of reasons he might have for actually deciding to accept this way of live. Here "reasons" would perhaps not be the best word to use. "Motivations" would be more appropriate. Such motivations for decision could be a personal attraction born in a person for Christ in reading about him in the New Testament about the lives of those who lived his teachings. It may be the agonizing realization of the relativeness and temporality of the purely empirical world and thus finding in the Christian way of life an answer to the anguished search for an anchoring of one's existence. It may be the edification gained in observing the unselfish lives of the Christians, of one's teachers, parents and loved ones.

In the case of one who already follows the Christian way of live, the occasions for unuttered justification for the Christian assertions may come in time of temptations against the faith or in time of any other existential difficulty. In the former case, when he is tempted to doubt this or that article of belief, he might use Scripture, the expert opinion of theologians or the authority of the Church as reasons for adhering to them in spite of their opaqueness. Or he might try to clarify it by reflection on it, using other belief utterances to discern its meaning. He might try to resolve his doubts during situations of crisis by relying on the most fundamental of creedal assertions, namely, the first article of the creed: "I believe in God, the Father Almighty." Such limit situations need not always be negative ones. Experiences of self-transcending love, of ecstatic happiness, of overwhelming joy, can give him insights into the meaningfulness of believing in one or the other creedal utterance, for example, in the one already mentioned about God being a loving Father. In this case, however, one cannot properly talk of "giving reasons for one's creedal affirmations." "seeing a sense in believing creedal statements" would be more appropriate.

Aside from limit situations, there are other more ordinary occasions when a believer finds it necessary to give reasons for creedal assertions. A most normal and ordinary occasion is when parents give religious instructions to their children. When the children are still small, arguments on authority may predominate over other reasons and as the children grow up, the reasonability intrinsic to individual creedal statements may increasingly be made use of.

Another occasion is when one wishes to assure oneself or comfort others in time of sorrow. A wife who has deep faith, losing a beloved husband, answers expression of condolences of close friends with: "I believe that we shall once again be united in God, because such a love as ours cannot have an end." A person who had gone through many reverses but has gained a certain mastery of life through these sufferings, writes consolingly to one who has just suffered a bitter disappointment thus:

> Ich glaube, daß Gott wirklich unser Vater ist, weil ich oft im Leben erfahren habe, daß er alles zum Guten führt. Für Dich ist diese Erfahrung sicher auf die Dauer heilsam und segensreich. Denn das Bittere, das zunächst enttäuscht, ist auf die Dauer oft besser und bringt eher wahres Glück als das Gegenteil.[21]

Dallas High cites yet another reason given for belief in the first article of the Apostles' Creed thus:

> For a creedal utterance such as "I believe in God, the Father Almighty" or the corresponding doctrinal expression "God is our Father," I (we) can give "reason," "justification," or an "anchor" for my (our) saying or laying claim to the belief... The "anchor" or "reason" may be, for example, of the following kind: "I was extremely ill last month, but now, thank God, I am completely well."[22]

Another occasion when a believer gives reasons for creedal utterances is when he is challenged about his belief utterances either belligerently or because of interest on the part of others to find out why he adheres to his belief. In these occasions, the believer tends to give reasons which could be accepted or grasped by those who do not have the same presupposi-

---

21 From a private letter.
22 D. High, *Language, Persons and Belief*, 210.

tions as he, but who at least share with him the common ground of rationality and humanness. Among people of the same presuppositions, he likewise engages in the activity of giving reasons for creedal affirmations, i.e. in dialogues. But usually here, aside from the kind of reasons cited in the previous sentence, he likewise makes much use of reasons which are understandable to both parties, because of common basic presuppositions held by them. For example, to the non-believer, he would justify the creedal claims about Christ on historical grounds, the impact he has had on men of all times, etc. To another believer with whom he discusses the same topic, he would use the prophecies of the Old Testament, the testimony of the apostles, the authority of the Church, the opinion of theologians, and so on.

The activity of giving reasons for one's belief finds a sytematization in the hands of the theologians, whose profession it is to reflect on matters of faith. But whether done by a layman or by a theologian, it is to be observed that the anchorings given for belief take on many forms - empirical anchorings, anchorings in authority, anchorings in history, in testimony, existential anchorings, and so forth. These reasons may, furthermore, be classified roughly into "truth discerning" reasons which are reasons that can "count toward establishing the truth of the assertions,"[23] and "decisional" reasons meaning those which justify one's personal choice to affirm or to adhere the creedal assertions. The latter type includes the former but goes beyond it, because for a choice, factors other than the objective truth can play a role.

That these reasons are weighty enough to appeal to the human mind is shown by the high stakes believers risk on the assertions they justify. The recognition of this fact is one of Wittgenstein's rare insights which he expresses thus: "This (religious discourse belief), in one sense, must be called the firmest of all beliefs, because the man risks things on account of it, which he would not do on things which are better established for him."[24]

An examination of the reasons cited in this section shows that these are still within the presuppositions of the Christian way of life. In lin-

---

[23] Diogenes Allen, *The Reasonableness of Faith* (Washington: Corpus Books, 1968), xviii.

[24] L. Wittgenstein, *Lectures and Conversations*, 54.

guistic terms, they are still within the grammar of Christian religious discourse. The convert's reflection whether to adopt the Christian way of life or not comes closest to the justification of the system as a whole and therefore already touches in some way the external justification of the system. But it does not exhaust the reasons falling under this external justification. So the question remains: "Why does it make sense to speak the Christian religious discourse at all?" The following section will discuss this question.

IV. *The Significance of Christian Religious Discourse*

The treatment of the external justification of Christian religious discourse brings the discussion to the very rock bottom of language. Human language as such is indispensible to man. If one is born a man, he must speak human language. But the question is: Must he speaks this or that particular language game? Is there any specific form of discourse that he must of necessity adopt? Or is his speaking of particular forms of discourse conditioned by factors such as concrete historical circumstances and by his choice of those forms of discourse which he deems important to his human existence?

The analogy of playing games can serve a purpose at this point. There is, as such, no particular game which must necessarily be played by any man. In fact man need never play any game at all, although a man who never played a game in his life will probably not be the most human of men. Here is where the analogy limps. But it has a "sound leg" which can here be considered, because it will be helpful in the discussion. This consists in a way man chooses the specific games he plays. In his choice, he is influenced first of all by the availability of games in his geographical environment and by his acquaintance with these games. His choice is, furthermore, not dictated by logical necessity but by his seeing a value or values in specific games which is, of course, conditioned by his own capacity to play them. Consequently if one were to convince him to play a particular game, one would have to show him a game actually being played, taking care to explain to him all the different moves and all the other aspects involved in it, hoping that these will appeal to his interest and to his judgement to such an extent that he will consider playing this game as a profitable way of spending his leisure time.

The analogy as applied to the language game of Christian religious discourse is, as has been said, imperfect, but it serves the purpose of indicating the manner in which it can be justified. Unlike games, human language is indispensible to man. But like specific games, the specific language games are chosen, not in virtue of their intrinsic indispensibility, but in view of concrete circumstances and the free decision of the individual. If it is true that no specific form of discourse must by necessity be spoken, then the justification of the Christian religious discourse will resemble the justification of any other form of discourse and this will go along the lines taken by the justification of specific games. There is, however, an important difference which distinguishes the Christian religious discourse both from games and from other forms of discourse. No game claims to appeal to the whole of man's existence, nor even to the most vital aspects of human life. Its appeal, though not negligible, is limited. Thus the activity of justifying games, although useful, is relatively unimportant.

Some other forms of discourse, like poetry, scientific discourse, aesthetic talk, and so on, do claim to appeal to some very important aspects of being human. In today's technical world, it is almost unthinkable for the great majority of men to ignore scientific discourse in its various forms, because on it depends Man's physical survival. No one would deny the impoverishment of the human spirit, if he could no longer articulate himself in poetry, in art, or in music. But it remains that they do not claim the whole of man's existence and the one or the other person can be excused for refusing to "dabble in poetry" or for not giving art, music or theoretical science an important place in his life.

Christian religious discourse, however, claims to appeal not only to a part of man's existence or to some important aspects of it; it claims to give meaning to the whole of man's life, and not only to this or that man's life, but to that of every man. Confronted with such a claim, the question is: Would it not be utter stupidity, or at least irresponsible levity for a man who takes his existence seriously, to refuse a serious consideration of it? But for Christian religious discourse to merit such a consideration, it must be able to show itself worthy of such an attention. The following paragraphs will discuss such a possibility.

The task of justifying Christian religious discourse is tantamount to giving a justification for its basic presuppositions, which are the foundations of its being the kind of language game that it specifically is. The most basic presupposition of Christian religious discourse, as has been pointed out in the preceding chapter, is the *theistic presupposition*, which is articulated by theistic propositions. The task here is therefore to show the credentials of theistic propositions.

Theistic assertions, it is to be remembered, are creedal, and not empirical assertions. Any attempt to treat them separately from their character as belief statements will find them unintelligible, because one cannot use the criterion of confirmability/incomfirmability which is indispensible in the treatment of empirical factual statements. Theistic propositions have essentially another function, namely, to articulate certain human experiences which are beyond the competence of empirical factual statements to express, because they involve those aspects of being human, which, although they manifest themselves within the concrete world, nevertheless escape an exact pinpointing within its coordinate system. This involves the more elusive human faculties of will and emotions. For the giving of good reasons for God-talk and consequently of religious discourse, it is necessary to take into account the role of these non-intellective aspect of faith, namely the affective and the volitional.

In the discussions concerning the theistic propositions among philosophers of religion, there have been significant dichotomies which pitted the discussants one against the other: cognitive-emotive, objective-subjective, descriptive-conative, assertive-commissive, factual-grammatical, etc. These dichotomies have caused a polarization which has for a long time prevented an adequate treatment of theistic statements. They have given the discussions a polemical character with the offensive and defensive moves played before the tribunal of reason,[25] the verdict being another dichotomy - rational-irrational. This is, consciously or unconsciously, interpreted as acceptable or not acceptable, because whether one admits or not, the reign of Mirabella, the goddess of reason enthroned in the Age of Enlightenment, has not yet quite ended. There is a need for the so-called "Aufklärung" to be itself "aufgeklärt" and this is no where so essential as in the discussion of religious discourse. This is not a flight to irrationalism, because it is reason itself that has to do this enlightenment and this consists in its recognition of its own limitation and of its need of the other

---

25 "Reason" is here used to mean "discursive reason."

human faculties to grasp reality. This is to say that between the "rational" and the "irrational" there is a vast area of unexplored territory of the "non-rational" which seems to give an account of the most profound phenomena of human existence. In recent discussions, more and more thinkers are recognizing the importance of taking this into account. Dennis O'Brien, for example, writes:

> I would suggest that one of the reasons that "person" has become such a central category in modern theological discussions is that it has become clear that the "reality" with which the theologian is concerned is not one that cannot be grasped immediately by reason or argued by reason... When the theologian says that reason is incompetent to do this job, he should be understood to be making a judgement about the specific functions and capabilities of reason as contrasted with some other faculty or factulties. If, however, reason is understood as a blanket term for the sound functioning of our mental capacities, then one who attacks the competence of reason is committing himself not to the Church but to the asylum.[26]

In characterizing theistic propositions as authentic articulations of reality, the thing to do when confronted with the dilemma post by the previous mentioned dichotomies, is not to take either this or that horn of the dilemma, but to grasp both. Theistic propositions, as has been said, are necessarily belief propositions. In our analysis of "belief" and "belief statements," we have sufficiently shown that their grammar includes both alternatives of the dichotomies: they are both cognitive and emotive (volitional); both subjective and objective; descriptive and non-descriptive; assertive and commissive; factual and grammatical; and some statements are verifiable and others not. Furthermore, in giving account of theistic propositions as linguistic expressions that are to be taken seriously, no attempt will be made to prove them to be true. *Christian religious discourse does not depend on a proved existence of God but on a serious belief of God's reality.*

In the last chapter's discussion on the meaning of creedal statements, it has been shown that theistic propositions have intelligible or cognitive aspects in that they have a referent, which although not ostensible nor clearly de-limited, is, nevertheless definite enough to be talked about. Theistic propositions, likewise, make serious truth claims which are not

---

26 D. O'Brien, "On the Limitations of Reason" in John Hick (ed.), *Faith and the Philosophers* (London: Macmillan and Co. Ltd., 1964), 233 ff.

backed up by scientific verification but by the risk and commitment of those who utter them. And the reason for considering this "backing up" acceptable in determining the seriousness of the truth claims, is the fact that these propositions go beyond the aspects of reality which appeals exclusively to theoretical reason. In other words, theistic propositions do not claim to be *fully* cognitive. If they did, they would indeed be meaningless, because they could possibly not give a full rational account of their claims in the sense of rationality as "abstract theoretical operation of the intellect, with mathematics as the paradigmatic case."[27] Strange to say, their cognitivity (intelligibility) lies in the fact that they are also non-cognitive (non-intellectual), *that they express dimensions of human experience that are missed by the purely abstract kind of thinking*. To give an imperfect but telling analogy: A man would be considered irrational, if he insisted on acting always and only according to strict logical syllogisms.

A treatment of these realms of human existence which go beyond perception and intellection is necessary to show the significance of theistic propositions.

The *Christian* theistic propositions have as their subject, The God of the Christian, who is not automatically to be identified with the Being talked about by philosophers, nor even with the God of Abraham, Isaac and Jacob. The attributes of these concepts may, likewise, be found in the Christian concept of God, but this has a unique and important qualification. *The God of the Christian is the "Father of our Lord Jesus Christ."* Christian theistic propositions are therefore inseparably bound with the Christiological assertions which articulates the experience of Christ. The emotive, volitional and other non-rational factors entering into these propositions gain a definiteness not given in the creedal characterizations of religious experience expressed in the following varying formulations: "the power of the wholly other" (G. van der Leeuw); "the feeling of absolute dependence" (Schleiermacher); the "experience of the ultimate" (Tillich); "the need for social stability" (Malinowsky); "the experience of the sacred" (M. Eliade); "the creature feeling before the Numinous" (R. Otto); "the sense of wonder" (Chesterton and H. Graef); "the need for salvation" (D. Allen); "the experience of loving and being loved" (H.H. Price); "the encounter

---

27 J. Macquarrie, *Principles of Christian Theology* (London: SCM Press, 1966), 50.

with the Thou" (M. Buber).[28]

All these may also be found in the Christian religious experience, but in it, these non-reational characterizations of human experience which become verbalized in theistic statements, are encountered in relation to a concrete historical person - in Jesus Christ of Nazareth. The Christian theistic propositions are grounded in a concrete history. They are the articulations of the impact of a man, who, by his life and words, by his impossibly radical claims and by his irreproachable life, brought the people whom he met into a situation of "crisis" - into a situation of decision, either to consider him as a dangerous fool or to take seriously and believe that to which his whole being was a revelation and witness - the reality which enclosed not only his own person but someone he called "Father," whose "will" was the main criterion of his acts.

History shows that those, who decided against him, acted accordingly and put him to death and the others, who chose to believe in him, saw a confirmation of their choice in subsequent events, in their experience of him as "having risen from the dead." In the attempt to put into words their overwhelming experiences, they developed a form of discourse, which today is characterized as Christian. These Christian creedal propositions are not justifiable as informative description of states of affairs. They are intelligible and acceptable as verbalizations of a communal experience of a personal encounter and have the same status as any linguistic attempt to articulate human experiences that go beyond discursive categorization.

These propositions form the framework, within which the meaning and significance of the multi-dimensional activities involved in the Christian way of life are to be located. The explanation and interpretation of these activities belong to the task of the different branches of Christian theology. The demonstration of how they are actually lived is the duty and

---

[28] Cf. G. van der Leeuw, *Religion in Essence and Manifestation* (London: Allen and Unwin Ltd., 1938); F. Schleiermacher, *On Religion: Speeches to its Cultured Despisers* (New York: Harper and Row, 1958); P. Tillich, *Theology of Culture* (New York: OUP, 1964); B. Malinowsky, *Magic, Science and Religion* in J. Needham, ed. *Science, Religion and Reality* (London: SPCR, 1925); M. Eliade, *The Sacred and the Profane* (New York: Harcourt Brace and World, 1959); M. Buber, *I and Thou* (New York: Charles Scribners' Sons, 1958); R. Otto, *The Idea of the Holy* (New York: Oxford University Press, 1946); H. Graef, *Adult Christianity* (Chicago, Illinois: Franciscan Herald Press, 1965); Diogenes Allen, *The Reasonableness of Faith* (Washington: Corpus Books, 1968); H.H. Price, "Faith and Belief" in Hick, ed. *Faith and the Philosophers*, 3-25.

privilege of the Christian community. All these three factors: the justification of the basic presuppositions of the Christian way of life; the explanation and interpretation of the activities involved in it; the demonstration of how it is actually lived, all belong to an adequate justification of Christian religious discourse, as has been pointed out in the beginning of this section. It is obviously impossible for this thesis to tackle the last two of these factors. It is only the first task which belongs to its competence and therefore it serves only as a *starting point* for the actual and adequate justification of Christian religious discourse.

It must be noted that in justifying the basic Christian presuppositions, no attempt was made to prove them true nor to render them self-evident. It only attempted to show that these assumptions are anchored in human experiences and therefore can be the basis of a way of life that is engaged in by human beings. Consequently, the Christian religious discourse, which is the linguistic expression of this way of life, finds its significance in its attempt to articulate these experiences. Perhaps it does so imperfectly. Perhaps compared to what it wants to express, it is mere stutterings. It is, at least, an alternative to silence, and where silence better expresses what it wants to say imperfectly, it should perhaps keep quiet. It cannot claim to be the universal language of humanity, because that which it expresses might be expressed in some other ways. However, it offers enough appeal to man's faculties - rational, emotive, and volitional, to warrant its being taken seriously and its being chosen as the utterance of one's existence. It does not have the cercive force of obvious nor the inescapable consequence of the logically necessary. To engage in Christian religious Discourse remains a free choice, but a choice which is neither arbitrary nor irrational, but a decision based on acceptable grounds.

CONCLUSION

Coming to an end brings one inevitably to the beginning. When reflection has come to a full circle, it finds itself at the starting point, which invites it to run the course once again, and then again in a never ending, ever deepening process of understanding. So, as this thesis reaches its conclusion, it is set on a course of recapitulation. In this process, conclusions will be drawn from the first and more detailed reflection set down in the previous chapters and will be stated as clearly and succinctly as possible in this concluding chapter. This section will also point out the extent of originality in content and method of this thesis which justifies it as a doctoral study.

The dissertation undertook the task of understanding the linguistic act of "confessing one's belief" by analysing creedal statements. As a historical background for this study, the first chapter made an evaluative survey of the varied linguistic analyses of religious language beginning with the verificational analysis of the logical positivists which completely invalidated religious language and pronounced it meaningless according to empiristic criteria of meaning. The stimulated philosophical atmosphere created by this bold challenge gave rise to other forms of linguistic analysis of religious language. The immediate reaction was the non-cognitive analysis which accepted the positivistic presuppositions, but pointed out various other aspects of religious language ignored by the positivists. This, however, tended to reduce religious propositions to their non-cognitive aspects which subsequent groups of analysts undertook to correct by emphasizing the descriptive-cognitive character of these propositions. Further developments in linguistic analysis gave rise to a more recent group which rejected the positivistic presuppositions and refused to enter into the non-cognitive debate, but instead set out to understand religious propositions in their actual uses.

This critical survey, aside from providing a background for this study, likewise influenced its own analysis by showing, negatively, where such analysis could reach a dead-end, and positively, by opening up possibilities of a more constructive analysis of religious propositions. It has, in fact, provided this study with the opportunity to discern the methods that seemed to yield most fruit.

The combination of the Wittgensteinian approach and the Austinian method of statement analysis is the first claim to originality this thesis makes. The recent treatment of religious language has taken largely the Wittgensteinian approach. Dallas High is its most outstanding exponent. Donald Evans can be considered as the pioneer in adopting Austin's idea of performative language in the analysis of theological concepts. After him, there has not been any published work making use of the same method.[1] A combination of the two methods in analysing creedal discourse, is, to the best knowledge of the writer, not yet attempted. This combination was chosen, because it was seen to provide a complementary treatment of the creedal discourse. The Wittgensteinian approach located it in its proper context and enabled one to trace it contours broadly on the map of human language and more sharply on that of religious discourse. The Austinian method of statement analysis complemented this approach by giving an internal aspect to the treatment of creedal discourse, by disclosing the forces of creedal statements as speech acts which helped to relate them to other forms of discourse from another angle.

The concentration on creedal statements is not original, is not unique to this thesis. Linguistic analysts of religious language have focused their attention on these statements, sensing that these form the kernel of religious language. A second claim to originality can be made at this point, because what the linguistic analysts sensed and presupposed but did not show, i.e. the central role of creedal statements in religious discourse, has been shown in the third and fourth chapter of this work. This necessitated the treatment of the creedal statements as speech acts in varying forms, imbedded in a concrete way of life - the Christian way of life, having served various functions in a specific tradition - in the Christian

---

[1] In the University of Augsburg, Germany, Prof. Bernhard Casper is working on Austin's idea of performatives in the treatment of theological statements, but he has, up to the writing of this thesis, not yet published his work.

tradition. This has given a concrete and practical dimension to the often abstract, theoretical and isolated treatment of these statements so far done by linguistic analysts. The disclosure of the varied impulses to creedal utterances and their corresponding forces, showing them to be constituted by differing speech acts, has broken the dichotomies (descriptive-evaluative; cognitive-emotive, etc.) which have blocked philosophical and theological discussions and have given them a polemical character.

The difficult task of comparing creedal statements with other forms of discourse within human language and with other language games within Christian religious discourse appears likewise to have, as yet, no precedence. This lack of precedence was, in fact, the greatest difficulty felt in writing this thesis.

In the discussion of the "meaning" of creedal statements in Chapter V, which took its cue from Wittgenstein's definition as "meaning" as "use," a remark of Stuart Brown concerning the "grammatical function" of articles of faith[2], has been blown up into an explanation of the role of creedal statements in the Christian religious discourse, which is, hopefully, plausible and helpful to the understanding of these statements and provocative of new attitudes towards them.

Chapter VI grew out of the insights both of Chapter IV and V. In the comparison of creedal discourse with other forms of human discourse, the altogether remarkable affinity which accredits creedal statements as legitimate members of the family of human discourse, are nevertheless put into question by the radically unique character of their referent. It was felt that a justification other than the actuality of Christian creedal discourse was called for. Furthermore, a nuance of "meaning", i.e. as "significance" was left undiscussed in Chapter V, because it was in some way connected with the bigger task of giving reasons or justifying creedal statements. Keeping in mind that creedal statements characterized and distinguished Christian religious discourse, and that this discourse is the articulation of a specific way of life, the discussions both of justification of creedal statements and of the significance of Christian religious discourse were located in the treatment of the "form of life" of creedal statements.

What are the main insights into creedal statements gained in this study?

---

2 Stuart Brown, *Do Religious Claims Make Sense*, 147.

First of all, the survey made of the uses of the creed in the Christian tradition, has shown that creedal statements are the crystallization not only of *one* speech act, but of several speech acts which differ according to their varied uses in different contexts. The investigation of the forces of creedal statements has shown that these statements have both a performative and a constative aspect. They are *characteristically* and *distinctively* "performing statements," but their performance is necessarily grounded on their descriptive claims and therefore on their constative aspect. As performative statements, they exhibit different illocutionary forces according to their specific uses. Baptismal creeds, creeds used in the liturgy, and spontaneous creedal utterances exhibit primarily behabitive and commissive forces; synodal creeds show verdictive and exercitive forces; declaratory creeds and theological creedal statements are mainly expositive in force.

The comparison of creedal statements with the other religious uses of language located creedal statements in the very heart of Christian religious discourse. They constitute its distinguishing factor from non-religious uses of language on the one hand, and on the other, they ground and give meaning to other forms of speech acts within Christian religious discourse, such as prayer, preaching, theological statements, doctrinal pronouncements, and so on. They state the prime presuppositions of Christian religious discourse and exercise a grammatical function within it.

Reflection on creedal statements in the context of a specific way of life has shown that they are linguistic attempts to articulate human experiences that cannot be exhausted by words. They gain meaning and significance in a specific human form of life. The criterion of their meaning is found in the Christian way of life and as long as this form of life persists, no school of thought can validly refute the legitimacy of Christian religious discourse as its form of articulation. But because the reality it articulates is neither self-evident nor logically necessary, it cannot force anyone to speak it. Creedal statements have, therefore, a *decisional* character and their utterance involves the exercise of human freedom.

Some consequences follow from these insights which are relevant both in the field of Philosophy of Religion and in the theological discipline. The multi-dimensional character of the creed affects the discussions in the Philosophy of Religion, showing that an abstract, one-dimensional treatment of creedal statements, detached from their concrete uses in specific contexts, misrepresent or at best give only a partial view of these statements.

Theology can profit from the dissolution of the cognitive-emotive, descriptive-evaluative dichotomies concerning creedal statements by turning its attention away from fruitless polemics about these and spending its efforts at adopting the insights of linguistic analysis in its own reflections. For this, it is perhaps not un-called for to keep reminding theologians that linguistic analysis is not synonymous with logical-positivistic analysis to which they are understandably not receptive. The survey done in Chapter II of this work has shown, that there are other more constructive methods based on other presuppositions, which can help the theologian in clarifying religious concepts.

It is also to be hoped that this study has contributed to the effort at dissuading those theologians, who still insist on proving the claims of creedal statements as though they were as self-evident as logical statements or as demonstrable as scientific statements, from going on with these futile undertakings. To use metaphysical arguments to establish the kind of certainty demanded by logicians and scientists about creedal statements is as absurd as Gagarin's using empirical means to prove the contrary. There is a need of breaking out of the confining presuppositions of logical positivism and the one-dimensional view of language, on which the efforts of some exponents of Natural Theology are consciously or unconsciously based.

It still remains to show how this study has opened up further areas of research. Chapter IV, which attempted to compare and contrast creedal statements with other forms of discourse, reveals a vast area of investigation. Each set of comparison, not only between creedal statements and other forms of discourse (i.e. creedal statements-scientific statements), but also between the different forms of discourse (i.e. poetic discourse-philosophical discourse), can be a topic of a doctoral dissertation. Similar studies such as that undertaken by this work, focusing on the other uses of religious language such as prayer, preaching, dogmatic pronouncement, etc., could be fruitful contributions to the understanding of Christian religious discourse. For Theology, this would mean a deepening of the understanding of the phenomenon of faith; for Philosophy, this could result in an ever greater clarification of the different forms of speech acts and therefore of the workings of language as a whole. Even as regards creedal discourse, this work does not claim to have said the last word. On the contrary, it sees itself as a starting point for further investigations of the different forces of creedal statements. Having located the speech acts involved in the linguistic act of "confessing one's belief" in their proper context, it envisions the possibility of analysing the individual articles of the creed in a similar manner, thus disclosing nuances that may still lie undiscovered in creedal statements.

BIBLIOGRAPHY

Note: The bibliographical entries concerning the linguistic analysis of religious language include not only those actually used in this work. Effort was expanded toward completeness so as to provide help for future work of this type. The entries for the other sections are, however, selective.

I. ON CREEDS

BOOKS:

Barth, Karl. *Credo*. Zürich: Evangelischer Verlag, 1946.

Crehan, J. *Early Baptism and Creed*. London: Burns and Oates, 1950.

Cullmann, O. *Die ersten christlichen Glaubensbekenntnisse*. tr. by Hans Schaffert. Zürich: Evangelischer Verlag, 1943.

Curtis, William. *A History of Creeds and Confessions of Faith*. Edinburgh: T & T Clark, 1911.

Denzinger-Schönmetzer. *Symbolorum definitionum et declarationum de rebus fidei er morum*. Barcinone: Herder, 1967.

Fuhrmann, Paul. An *Introduction to the Great Creeds of the Church*. Philadelphia: The Westminster Press, 1969.

Hahn, August. *Bibliothek der Symbole und Glaubensregeln der alten Kirche*. Breslau: Morgenstern, 1897.

Kattenbusch, Ferdinand. *Das apostolische Symbol, sein geschichtlicher Sinn, seine ursprüngliche Stellung in Kultur und in der Theologie der Kirche*. Leipzig: J.C. Hinrichs'sche Buchhandlung, 1894-1900.

Lehmann, Karl et al. *Veraltetes Glaubensbekenntnis?* Regensburg: Verlag Friedrich Pustet, 1968.

Macdonald, Alexander. *The Apostles' Creed*. London: Kegan Paul, Trench Trubner & Co., Ltd., 1925.

Neufeld, Vernon. *The Earliest Christian Confessions*. Leiden: E.J. Brill, 1963.

Ratzinger, Josef. *Einführung in das Christentum*. München: Kösel Verlag, 1968.

Schillebeeckx, E. *Offenbarung und Theologie*. Mainz: Matthias-Grünewald Verlag, 1965. Particular attention to the chapter, "Das Glaubenssymbol und Theologie," 163-174.

Steubing, Hans, et.al. (eds.) Bekenntnis der Kirche. Wuppertal: Theologischer Verlag Rolf Brockhaus, 1970.

Wensinck, A.J. *The Muslim Creed*. Cambridge: University Press, 1932.

ARTICLES:

"Bekenntnis," in *Die Religion in Geschichte und Gegenwart*, I, 1957, cols. 988-1017.

Camelot, P.T. "Symbola" in *Sacramentum Mundi*, 1st. ed., IV, 790-795.

Curtis, Wiliam. "Confessions" in *The Encyclopedia of Religion and Ethics*, 1st ed., III, 831-892.

Semmelroth, Otto. "Kurzformel des Glaubens und ihr Sitz im Leben" in *Geist und Leben*. XLIV (1971), 440-452.

Rahner, Karl. "Pluralism in Theology and the Unity of the Church's Profession of Faith" in *Concilium*, VI (1969), 49-58.

Rahner und Lehmann. "Die Forderung nach einer 'Kurzformel' des christlichen Glaubens" in *Concilium*, III (1967), 203-207.

UNPUBLISHED MATERIAL:

Fransen, Piet. "Unity and Confessional Statements" copy of a lecture. (Photocopy), 1-34.

II. METHODOLOGY

TEXTS:

Austin, John L. *How To Do Things With Words*. ed. J.O. Urmson. London: Oxford University Press, 1967.

- *Philosophical Papers*. ed. J.O. Urmson and G.J. Warnock. London: Oxford University Press, 1970.

- *Sense and Sensibilia*. London: Oxford University Press, 1962.

Wittgenstein, Ludwig. *Philosophical Investigations*. Oxford: Basil Blackwell, 1953.

- *Tractatus Logico-Philosophicus*. Frankfurt am Main: Suhrkamp Verlag, ^{6}1960.

- *Über Gewissheit*. Frankfurt am Main: Suhrkamp Verlag, 1970.
- *Lectures and Conversations on Aesthetics, Psychology and Religious Belief*. ed. Cecil Barrett. Oxford: Basil Blackwell, 1966.

SECONDARY LITERATURE:
BOOKS:

Black, Max. *A Companion to Wittgenstein's Tractatus*. Cambridge: University Press, 1954.

Fann, Kuang Tih. *Symposium on Austin*. London: Routledge and Kegan Paul, 1969.
- *Wittgenstein's Conception of Philosophy*. Los Angeles: University of California Press, 1969.

Furberg, Mats. *Saying and Meaning*. Oxford: Basil Blackwell, 1971.

Hudson, Donald. *Ludwig Wittgenstein*. London: Lutterworth Press, 1968.

Pears, David. *Wittgenstein*. London: Fontana/Collins, 1971.

Pitcher, George. *The Philosophy of Wittgenstein*. Englewood Cliffs, N.J.: Prentice-Hall, 1964.
- (ed.) *Wittgenstein, The Philosophical Investigations*. New York: Doubleday & Co., 1966.

Wisdom, John. *Paradox and Discovery*. Oxford: Basil Blackwell, 1965.

ARTICLES:

Bell, Richard. "Wittgenstein and Descriptive Theology" in *Religious Studies*. V (1969), 1-18.

Cavell, Stanley. "Austin at Criticism" in Rorty, Richard. *The Linguistic Turn: Recent Essays in Philosophical Method*. Chicago and London: The University of Chicago Press, 1967, 239-247.

Dilman, Ilham. "On Wittgenstein's Last Notes: On Certainty, (1950-1951)" in *Philosophy*, 76 (1971), 162-168.

Hampshire, Stuart. "J.L. Austin" in Rorty, Richard, *The Linguistic Turn*, 239-247.

Pears, David. "Wittgenstein and Austin" in B. Williams and A. Montefiori (eds.) *British Analytical Philosophy*. London: Routledge and Kegan Paul, 1966, 17-40.

Urmson, J.O. "John Langshaw Austin" in *Encyclopedia of Philosophy*. 1st. ed., I, 211-215.

Weitz, Morris. "Analysis Philosophical" in *Encyclopedia of Philosophy*, 1st. ed., I, 97-109.

UNPUBLISHED MATERIAL:

Hallett, Garth. "A Wittgensteinian Critique of Scientific Philosophy." Typewritten copy of a lecture. 1-15.

- "General Introduction to a Commentary on Wittgenstein's *Philosophical Investigations*." Typewritten manuscript. 1-48.

III. *ON LINGUISTIC ANALYSIS OF RELIGIOUS LANGUAGE*

BOOKS:

SINGLE WORKS:

Allen, Diogenes. *The Reasonableness of Faith*. Washington: Corpus Books, 1968.

Antiseri, Dario. *Filosofia analitica e semantica del linguaggio religioso*. Brescia: Queriniana, 1969.

Ayer, Alfred J. *Language, Truth and Logic*. London: Victor Gollancz, 1951.

Baillie, D.M. *God was in Christ*. London: Faber and Faber, 1948.

Baillie, J. *The Sense of the Presence of God*. New York: Charles Scribner's Sons, 1962.

Bendall, K. and Ferré, F. *Exploring the Logic of Faith*: A Dialogue on the Relation of Modern Philosophy to Christian Faith. New York: Association Press, 1962.

Blackstone, William. *Problem of Religious Knowledge*. Englewood Cliffs, N.J.: Prentice-Hall, 1963.

Bochenski, Josef. *The Logic of Religion*. New York: University Press, 1965.

Bodkin, M. *Studies of Type-Images in Poetry, Religion and Philosophy*. London: Oxford University Press, 1955.

Braithwaite, Richard. *An Empiricist's View of the Nature of Religious Belief*. Cambridge: University Press, 1955.

Brown, Stuart. *Do Religious Claims Make Sense?* London: SCM Press Ltd., 1969.

Buren, Paul van. *The Secular Meaning of the Gospel*. London: The Macmillan Co., 1963.

Calvelli-Adorno, Franz. *Über die religiöse Sprache: Kritische Erfahrungen*. Frankfurt am Main: Knecht, 1965.

Charlesworth, Maxwell. *Philosophy and Linguistic Analysis*. Pittsburgh: Duquesne University Press, 1959.
Christian, William. *Meaning and Truth in Religion*. New Jersey: Princeton University Press, 1959.
Cleobury, F.H. *Christian Rationalism and Philosophical Analysis*. London: James Clarke and Co., 1959.
Crystal, David. *Linguistics, Language and Religion*. New York: Hawthorn Books, 1965.
Daecke, Sigurd M. *Der Mythos vom Tode Gottes*. Hamburg: Furche Verlag, 1969.
Dilley, Frank B. *Metaphysics and Religious Language*. New York: Columbia University Press, 1964.
Evans, Donald. *Logic of Self-Involvement*. London: SCM Press, Ltd., 1963.
Farmer, H.H. *The World and God*. London: James Nisbet and Co., 1955.
Ferré, Frederick. *Basic Modern Philosophy of Religion*. London: Allen and Unwin, 1968.
- *Language, Logic and God*. London: Eyre & Spottiswoode, 1962.
Findlay, J.N. *Language, Mind and Value*. London: Allen and Unwin, 1963.
Flew, Antony. *God and Philosophy*. London: Hutchinson, 1966.
Foster, M.P. *Mystery and Philosophy*. London: SCM Press, Ltd., 1957.
Gellner, Ernest. *Words and Things. A Critical Account of Linguistic Philosophy and a Study in Ideology*. London: Victor Gollancz, Ltd., 1959.
Gilkey, Langdon. *Naming the Whirlwind: Renewal of God-Language*. Indianapolis: Bobbs Merril, 1969.
Hare, Richard M. *Freedom and Reason*. Oxford: At the Clarendon Press, 1963.
- *The Language of Morals*. London: University Press, 1952.
Hawkins, D.J.B. *The Essentials of Theism*. London: Sheed and Ward, 1949.
Heimbeck, R. *Theology and Meaning*. London: Allen and Unwin, 1969.
Hick, John. *Philosophy of Religion*. New Jersey, Englewood Cliffs: Prentice-Hall Inc., 1963.
Hodges, H.A. *Languages, Standpoints and Attitudes*. London: Oxford University Press, 1953.
Hordern, William. *Speaking of God*. New York: Macmillan Co., 1964.
Kimpel, B.F. *Language and Religion*. New York: Philosophical Library, 1957.
Ladriere, J. *L'articulation du sens*. Delachaux & Niestle, Desclée De Brouwer, 1970.
Laeuchli, Samuel. *The Language of Faith*. New York: Abingdon Press, 1962.

Lorenz, Kuno. *Elemente der Sprachkritik: Eine Alternative zum Dogmatismus und Skeptizismus in der analytischen Philosophie.* Frankfurt am Main: Suhrkamp Verlag, 1971.

Macquarrie, John. *God-Talk: An Examination of the Language and Logic of Theology.* London: SCM Press, 1967.

- *Principles of Christian Theology.* London: SCM Press, Ltd., 1966.

McIntyre, Alasdair. *Difficulties in Christian Belief.* London: SCM Press, Ltd., 1959.

Martin, James A. *The New Dialogue Between Philosophy and Theology.* New York: The Seabury Press, 1966.

Martin, C.B. *Religious Belief.* New York: Cornell University Press, 1959.

Mascall, E.L. *Existence and Analogy.* London: Longmans Green and Co., 1949.

Moreau, Jules. *Language and Religious Language.* Philadelphia: The Westminister Press, 1960.

Morra, G. *Il problema morale nel Neopositivismo.* Lacaita: Mandurai-Bati, Perugia, 1962.

Munz, Peter. *Problems of Religious Knowledge.* London: Student Christian Movement Press, 1959.

Ogden, Schubert M. *The Reality of God and other Essays.* New York: Harper, 1966.

Phillips, D.Z. *The Concept of Prayer.* London: Routledge and Kegan Paul, 1965.

- *Faith and Philosophical Enquiry.* London: Routledge and Kegan Paul, 1965.

Plantinga, Alvin. *God and other Minds.* New York and London: Oxford University Press, 1968.

Ross, James T. *Philosophical Theology.* Indianapolis: Bobbs Merril, 1969.

Ramsey, Ian T. *Christian Discourse: Some Logical Explorations.* London: Oxford University Press, 1965.

- *Miracles: An Exercise in Mapwork.* Oxford: At the Clarendon Press, 1952.
- *Models and Mystery.* London: Oxford University Press, 1964.
- *On Being Sure in Religion.* London: The Athlone Press, 1963.
- *Religious Language: An Empirical Placing of Theological Phrases.* London: SCM Press, Ltd., 1967.

Richmond, J. *Faith and Philosophy.* London: Hodder and Stoughton, 1966.

Robinson, N.H.G. *Faith and Duty.* London: Victor Gollancz, 1950.

Schmidt, Paul. *Religious Knowledge*. Glencoe, Illinois: The Free Press, 1961.

Smart, Ninian. *Reasons and Faith:An Investigation of Religious Discourse*. London: Routledge and Kegan Paul, 1958.

Urmson, J.O. *Philosophical Analysis*. Oxford: At the Clarendon Press, 1956.

Weiland, J.S. *New Ways in Theology*. Dublin: Gil and Macmillan, 1968.

Wicker, B. *God and Modern Philosophy*. London: Darton, Longman and Todd, 1964.

Williams, Bernard & Montefiori, Alan. *British Analytical Philosophy*. London: Routledge and Kegan Paul, 1966.

Wilson, James. *Language and Christian Belief*. London: Macmillan and Co., 1958.

Zuurdeeg, William F. *An Analytical Philosophy of Religion*. New York: Abingdon Press, 1958.

ANTHOLOGIES:

American Philosophical Association. *Proceedings of the Thirty-Fourth Annual Meeting*. Washington D.C., 1960.

Ammerman, Robert (ed.). *Classics of Analytical Philosophy*. New York: McGraw Hill, 1965.

Bowden J. and Richmond, J. (eds.) *A Reader in Contemporary Theology*. London: SCM Press, Ltd., 1967.

Feigl, H. and Sellars (eds.). *Readings in Philosophical Analysis*. New York: Appleton-Century Crofts, 1949.

Flew, Antony and MacIntyre, Alasdair (eds.). *New Essays in Philosophical Theology*. London: SCM Press, 1969.

Hartshorne, C. and Reese, W. (eds.). *Philosophers Speak of God*. London and Chicago: University of Chicago Press, 1953.

Hepburn, Ronald W. *Christianity and Paradox: Critical Studies in Twentieth Century Theology*. London: Watts, 1958.

Hick, John. (ed.) *Classical and Contemporary Readings in Philosophy of Religion*. Englewood Cliffs, N.J.: Prentice-Hall Inc., 1964.

- (ed.) *Faith and the Philosophers*. London: Macmillan and Co., 1964.

- (ed.) *The Existence of God*. New York and London: Macmillan Co., 1964.

- (ed.) *Faith and Knowledge*. New York: Cornell University Press, 1966.

High, Dallas (ed.) *New Essay in Religious Language.* New York: University Press, 1969.

Hook, S. (ed.) *Religious Experience and Truth: A Symposium.* New York: University Press, 1969.

Hutchinson, John A. *Language and Faith: Studies in Sign, Symbol and Meaning.* Philadelphia: Westminister Press, 1963.

Kiefer, H. and Munitz, Milton (eds.). *Language, Belief and Metaphysics.* Albany: State University of New York Press, 1970.

MacIntyre, Alasdair (ed.). *Metaphysical Beliefs: Three Essays.* London: SCM Press, Ltd., 1957.

Mitchell, Basil. (ed.) *Faith and Logic.* London: Allen and Unwin, 1957.

Phillips, D.Z. (ed.). *Religion and Understanding.* Oxford: Basil Blackwell, 1967.

Plantinga, Alvin (ed.). *The Ontological Argument from St. Anselm to Contemporary Philosophers.* Garden City: Doubleday and Co., 1965.

Ramsey, Ian T. (ed.). *Words About God: The Philosophy of Religion.* London: SCM Press, Ltd., 1971.

ARTICLES:

1. *Australasian Journal of Philosophy*

Boyce-Gibson, A. "Modern Philosophers Consider Religion" in *Australasian Journal of Philosophy*, XXXV (1957), 170-185.

Cameron, J.M. "R.F. Holland on Religious Discourse and Theological Discourse," in *Australasian Journal of Philosophy*, XXXIV (1956), 203-207.

Duff-Forbes, D.R. "Theology and Falsification Again," in *Australasian Journal of Philosophy*, XXXIX (1961), 143-154.

Flew, Antony. "Falsification and Hypothesis in Theology." *Australasian Journal of Philosophy*, XL (1962), 318-323.

Holland, R.F. "Modern Philosophers Consider Religion: A Reply." in *Australasian Journal of Philosophy*, XXXIV (1958), 208-209.

- "Religious Discourse and Theological Discourse." in *Australasian Journal of Philosophy*, XXXIV (1956), 147-163.

Horsburgh, H.J.N. "The Claims of Religious Experience." *Australasian Journal of Philosophy*, XXXV (1957), 186-200.

- "Professor Braithwaite and Billy Brown." *Australasian Journal of Philosophy*, XXXV (1957), 186-207.

Hudson, Donald. "Is God an Entity?" *Australasian Journal of Philosophy*, XLII (1964), 35-45.

Hutchings, P. "Discussion: Necessary Being." *Australasian Journal of Philosophy* XXXV (1957), 201-206.

Passmore, J. "Christianity and Positivism." *Australasian Journal of Philosophy*, XXXV (1957), 201-206.

Smart, J.J.C. "Philosophy and Religion." *Australasian Journal of Philosophy*, XXXVI (1958), 529-538.

2. *Christian Scholar, The*

Dirks, J.E. "The Relevance of Contemporary Analytic Philosophy for the Community of Christian Scholars." *The Christian Scholar*, 43 (1960), 251-265.

Ferré, F. "Mapping the Logic of Models in Science and Theology." *The Christian Scholar*, XLVI (1963), 3-39.

Gill, Jerry. "A Review of *Speaking of God* by William Hordern." *The Christian Scholar*, XLVII (1965), 320-323.

Tyson, R. "Philosophical Analysis and Religious Language." *The Christian Scholar*, XLIII (1960), 245-250.

3. *Journal of Philosophy*

Aldrich, Virgil, et. al. "The Sense of Dogmatic Religious Expression." *Journal of Philosophy*, LI (1954), 145-172.

Hick, J. "God as Necessary Being." *Journal of Philosophy*, LVII (1960), 725-732.

Matthews, G.B. "Theology and Natural Theology." *Journal of Philosophy*, LXL (1964), 99-108.

Nielsen, Kai. "On Talk About God." *Journal of Philosophy*, LV (1958), 888-890.

Schmidt, P. " Is there Religious Knowledge?" *Journal of Philosophy*, LV (1958), 529-538.

4. *Journal of Religion*

Boyce-Gibson, A. "Empirical Evidence and Religious Faith." *Journal of Religion*, XXXVI (1956), 24-35.

Flew, Antony. "Reflection of the Reality of God." *Journal of Religion*, XLVIII (1968), 150-161.

Gilkey, Langdon. "Cosmology, Ontology and the Travail of Biblical Language." *Journal of Religion*, XLI (1961), 194-201.

Klemke, E.D. "Are Religious Statements Meaningful?" *Journal of Religion*, XL (1960), 27-39.

Ogden, Schubert M. "God and Philosophy." *Journal of Religion*, XLVIII (1968), 161-181.

Thompson, S. "Philosophy and Theology: A Reply to Prof. W.F. Zuurdeeg." *Journal of Religion*, XL (1960), 9-17.

Zuurdeeg, W.F. "The Nature of Theological Language." *Journal of Religion*, XL (1960), 1-8.

5. *Mind*

Coval, S. "Worship Superlatives and Concept Confusion." *Mind*, LXVIII (1959), 218-222.

Cox, D. "The Significance of Christianity." *Mind*, LIX (1950), 209-218.

Evans, E.L. "On Meaning and Verification." *Mind*, LXIII (1953), 16-25.

Hepburn, R. "From World to God." *Mind*, LXXII (1963), 40-50.

Mcpherson, T. "The Existence of God," *Mind*, LIX (1950), 549-550.

Miles, T.R. "A Note on Existence." *Mind*, LX (1951), 399-402.

Nidditch, P. "A Defense of Ayer's Verifiability Principle Against Church Criticism." *Mind*, LXX (1961), 88-89.

6. *Philosophical Review, The*

Adams, M.M. "Is the Existence of God a 'Hard Fact'?" *The Philosophical Review*, LXXVI (1967), 492-503.

Alston, W. "Words and Images by Mascall - A Review." *The Philosophical Review*, LXIII (1959), 409-411.

Kennick, W. "The Language of Religion." *The Philosophical Review*, LXV (1956) 56-71.

Weitz, M. "Oxford Philosophy." *The Philosophical Review*, LXII (1953), 187-233.

7. *Philosophy*

Ewing, A.C. "Awareness of God." *Philosophy*, XL (1965), 1-17.

- "Religious Assertions in the Light of Contemporary Philosophy." *Philosophy*, XXXII (1957), 214-216.

Glasgow, W.E. "Knowledge of God." *Philosophy*, XXXII (1967), 229-240.

Hutchings, P. "Necessary Being and Some Types of Tautology." *Philosophy*, XXXIX (1964), 1-17.

Hartland-Swann, J. "What is Theology?" *Philosophy*, XXIX (1954), 54-64.

Inge, W.E. "Theism" *Philosophy* XXIII (1948), 54-65.

Lewis, H.D. "Contemporary Empiricism and the Philosophy of Religion." *Philosophy*, XXXII (1957), 193-205.

   - "What is Theology?" *Philosophy*, XXVII (1952), 345-358.

Nielsen, Kai. "Wittgensteinian Fideism." *Philosophy*, LXII (1967), 191-209.

8. *Philosophy and Phenomenological Research*

Demos, R. "The Meaningfulness of Religious Language." *Philosophy and Phenomenological Research*, XVIII (1957), 96-106.

Fitch, F. "On God and Immortality." *Philosophy and Phenomenological Research*, VIII (1948), 688-693.

9. *Proceedings of the Aristotelian Society*

Braithwaite, R.B. "The Nature of Believing." *Proceedings of the Aristotelian Society*, XXXIII (1933), 129-146.

Ewing, A.C. "Pseudo-Solutions." *Proceedings of the Aristotelian Society*, LVII (1956-57), 31-52.

Lewis, H.D. "The Cognitive Factor in Religious Experience." *Proceedings of the Aristotelian Society*, Supplementary Volume XXIX (1955), 59-84.

McPherson, T. "Assertions and Analogy." *Proceedings of the Aristotelian Society*, LX (1959-60), 155-170.

10. *Religious Studies*

Bell, R. "Wittgenstein and Descriptive Theology." *Religious Studies*, V (1969), 1-18.

Clifford, P. "The Factual Reference of the Theological Assertions." *Religious Studies*, III (1970), 339-346.

Coburn, R. "The Concept of God." *Religious Studies*, II (1966), 61-74.

Daher, A. "God and Factual Necessity." *Religious Studies*, VI (1970), 23-40.

Dilley, F. "An Analysis of J.J.C. Smart's Objections to the 'Proofs'." *Religious Studies*, IV (1969), 245-252.

Ewing, A.C. "Two Proofs of God's Existence." *Religious Studies*, L (1965), 29-45.

Findlay, J. "Logic of Mysticism." *Religious Studies*, II (1967), 145-162.

Gualtieri, A.R. "Truth Claims for Religious Images." *Religious Studies*, I (1966), 151-162.

Hall, R. "The Symbolic Relationship and Christian Truth." *Religious Studies*, II (1966), 129-136.

Henze, D.T. "Language Games and the Ontological Argument." *Religious Studies*, IV (1968), 147-152.

Hepburn, R.W. "Questions About the Meaning of Life." *Religious Studies*, I (1968), 125-140.

Heywood, T. "Religious Language as Symbolism." *Religious Studies*, I (1965), 89-94.

Langford, M. "The Problem of the Meaning of 'Miracle'." *Religious Studies*, VII (1970), 43-52.

Litzenburg, T.J. "Faith-In and In-Faith: A Reply to Prof. H.H. Price." *Religious Studies*, II (1967), 247-254.

Lockheed, D. "Is Existence a Predicate in Anselm's Argument?" *Religious Studies*, II (1966), 121-128.

MacCormac, E. "A New Programme for Religious Language: The Transformational Generative Grammar." *Religious Studies*, VI (1970), 41-56.

Miles, T.R. "On Excluding the Supernatural." *Religious Studies*, I (1966), 141-150.

Nielsen, K. "On Fixing the Reference Range of God." *Religious Studies*, II (1966), 13-36.

- "The Intelligibility of God-Talk." *Religious Studies*, VI (1970), 1-22.

Penelhum, T. "Divine Goodness and the Problem of Evil." *Religious Studies*, II (1966), 95-108.

Price, H.H. "On Believing: A Reply to Prof. R.W. Sleeper." *Religious Studies*, II (1967), 243-246.

Sleeper, R.C. "On Believing." *Religious Studies*, II (1966), 37-48.

Wainwright, W.J. "Religious Statements and the World." *Religious Studies*, II (1966), 49-60.

- "The Presence of Evil and the Falsification of Theistic Assertions." *Religious Studies*, IV (1969), 213-216.

11. *Other Journals*

Allison, H.E. "Faith and Falsifiability." *The Review of Metaphysics*, III (1969), 499-522.

Bortolaso, G. "Ludwig Wittgenstein: Linguaggio e metafisica." *La Civilta Cattolica*, 18, genn. 1969, 142-149.

Capizzi, A. "Ateismo e analisi del linguaggio nel pensiero inglese contemporaneo." *La Cultura*, IV (1966), 213-232.

Casey, J. "Speaking of God." *Continuum*, V (1967), 6-12.

Cossee de Maulde, G. "Analyse linguistique et langage religieux: L'approche de Ian Ramsey dans 'Religious Language'." *Nouvelle Revue Théologique*, 101e année, n. février, 199, 169-202.

Demonte, N. "Il linguaggio religioso oggi." *Opera Aperta*, III, 8-9, 1967.

Fisher, M. "Belief in God." *Methodos*, VIII (1961), 38-39.

Gill, J. "The Tacit Structure of Religious Knowing." *International Philosophical Quarterly*, IV (1969), 533-539.

Hartshorne, H.C. "John Wisdom on 'Gods'." *The Downside Review*, LXXVII (1959).

Hawkins, D.J.B. "What Do the Proof of the Existence of God Purport to Do?" *The Clergy Review*, XXXVII (1952), 321-331.

Hick, J. "The Idea of Necessary Being." *The Princeton Seminary Bulletin*, LIV (1960), 11-21.

- "Theology and Verification." *Theology Today*, XVII (1960), 15-17.

Huber, C. "Can We Still Speak About God?" *Gregorianum*, XLIX (1968), 4, 667 Ss.

Lewis, H.D. "Philosophers Survey X: The Philosophy of Religion." *Philosophical Quarterly*, IV (1954), 167-168.

Masterman, M. "Linguistic Philosophy and Dogmatic Theology." *Theology*, LIV (1951), 82-89.

Mondini, B. "Positivismo logico, analisi linguistica e teologia." *Divus Thomas*, LXIV (1961), 296-309.

Munk, O. "Zur Logik der Rede von Gott." *Zeitschrift für katholische Theologie*, 89 (1967), 1-28.

Nielsen, K. "Can Faith Validate God-Talk?" *Theology Today*, XX (1963), 158-173.

O'Meara, T. "Outlining the Problem." A Review of Macquarrie's "God-Talk." *Continuum*, V (1967), 583-586.

Phillips, D.Z. "Philosophical Theology and the Reality of God." *Philosophical Quarterly*, XII (1963).

Smith, R.V. "Analytical Philosophy and Religious-Theological Language." *Journal of Bible and Religion*, XXX (1962).

Vanni-Rovighi, S. "Filosofia analitica e religione." *Studium*, LXIV (1968), 743-751.

Weiss, P. "Religious Experience." *Review of Metaphysics*, XVII (1963), 3-17.

Williams, L. "God and Logical Analysis." *Downside Review*, LXXIV (1956).

IV. *OTHER SOURCES*

BOOKS:

Amiot, F. *History of the Mass*. London:Burns and Oates, 1959.

Berger, P. *The Sacred Canopy: Elements of a Sociological Theory of Religion*. Garden City: Doubleday and Co. Inc., 1969.

Hawkins, D.J.B. *The Concepts of Aesthetics*. London: Aquin Press, 1962.

Holländischen Bischöfe, Die. *Glaubensverkündigung für Erwachsene*. Deutsche Ausgabe des holländischen Katechismus. Nymegen-Utrecht: Dekker und Van de Vogt, 1966.

Hughes, P. *The Church in Crisis: A History of the General Councils, 325-1870*. Garden City: Hanover House, 1961.

James, W. *Varieties of Religious Experience: A Study of Human Nature*. New York: University Books, Inc. 1902.

Kunz, E. *Christentum ohne Gott*. Frankfurt am Main: Josef Knecht, 1971.

Loisy, A. *The Birth of the Christian Religion*. tr. by L.P. Jacks. New York: The Macmillan Co., 1948.

Müller, Max. (ed.) *The Sacred Books of the East*. vol. XXXI Oxford: At the Clarendon Press, 1887.

Ogden and Richard. *The Meaning of Meaning*. London: Routledge and Kegan Paul, 1952.

Oraison, M. *Strange Voyage: The Autobiography of a Non-Conformist*. Garden City:Doubleday and Co., Inc., 1970.

Pelikan, J. *The Christian Tradition: A History of Development of Doctrine*, I. *The Emergence of Catholic Tradition (100-600)*. Chicago and London: The University of Chicago Press, 1971.

Ruinart, Th. *Acta Martyrum*. Vienna: Rieger, 1803.

Schlink, E. *The Coming Christ and the Coming Church*. London and Edinburgh: Oliver Boyd, Ltd., 1967.

Therese of Lisieux. *Autobiography*. tr. by Ronald Knox. New York: P.S. Kenedy and Sons, 1958.

- *Geschichte einer Seele*. Trier: J. Zimmer Verlag, n.d.

ARTICLES:

Alfaro, J. "Faith." *Sacramentum Mundi*, 1968 ed. II, 310-322.

Latourelle, R. "Revelation, History and Incarnation." *The Word: Readings in Theology*. Innsbruck: P.J. Kenedy and Sons, 1964, pp. 27-57.

Rahner, K. "Dogma." *Sacramentum Mundi*, 1st.ed. II, 95-111.

- "Science as a 'Confession'?" in *Theological Investigations*, III. Baltimore: Helicon Press, 1967, 385-400.
- "What is a Dogmatic Statement?" *Theological Investigations*, V. Baltimore: Helicon Press, 1966, 42-66.

INTERVIEWS:

1. Prof. Karl Becker, Rome, October, 1972.
2. Fr. William Ellos, Rome, October, 1971.
3. Prof. Dorothy Emmet, Cambridge, Summer, 1971.
4. Prof. Heinrich Fries, Rome, March, 1972.
5. Prof. Garth Hallet, Rome, October, 1972.
6. Dr. Nicholas Lash, Cambridge, Summer, 1971.
7. Prof. Margaret Masterman, Cambridge, Summer, 1971.
8. Fr. Herbert Wutz, Rome, November, 1972.

APPENDIX

THE APOSTLES' CREED

Credo in Deum, Patrem omnipotentem, Creatorem caeli et terrae. Et in Jesum Christum, Filium ejus unicum, Dominum nostrum; qui conceptus est de Spiritu Sancto, natus ex Maria Virgine, passus sub Pontio Pilato, crucifixus, mortuus et sepultus: descendit ad inferos, tertia die resurrexit a mortuis, ascendit ad caelos, sedet ad dexteram Dei Patris omnipotentis, inde venturus est judicare vivos et mortuos. Credo in Spiritum Sanctum, sanctam Ecclesiam catholicam, Sanctorum communionem, remissionem peccatorum, carnis resurrectionem, vitam aeternam. Amen.

I believe in God the Father Almighty, Creator of heaven and earth. And in Jesus Christ, His only Son, Our Lord; who was conceived by the Holy Spirit, born of the Virgin Mary, suffered under Pontius Pilate, was crucified, died and was buried: He descended into hell, the third day He rose again from the dead, He ascended into heaven; sitteth at the right hand of God the Father Almighty, from thence He shall come to judge the living and the dead. I believe in the Holy Spirit, the Holy Catholic Church, the Communion of Saints, the forgiveness of sins, the resurrection of the body, and life everlasting. Amen.

THE NICENE CREED

Credo in unum Deum Patrem omnipotentem, factorem caeli et terrae, visibilium omnium et invisibilium.
Et in unum Dominum Jesum Christ-

I believe in one God the Father Almighty, maker of heaven and earth, and of all things visible and invisible.
And I believe in one Lord, Jesus

um, Filium Dei Unigenitum
Et ex Patre natum ante omnia
saecula
Deum de Deo
Lumen de lumine
Deum verum de Deo vero
Genitum, non factum, consubstantialem Patri; per quem omnia facta sunt.
Qui propter nos homines et propter nostram salutem descendit de caelis
Et incarnatus est de Spiritu Sancto ex Maria Virgine: Et homo factus est.
Crucifixus etiam pro nobis: sub Pontio Pilato passus et sepultus est.
Et resurrexit tertia die, secundum Scripturas
Et ascendit in caelum: sedet ad dexteram Patris
Et iterum venturus est cum gloria, judicare vivos et mortuos: cujus regni non erit finis.

Et in Spiritum Sanctum, Dominum et vivificantem
Qui ex Patre Filioque procedit

Qui cum Patre et Filio simul adoratur et conglorificatur
Qui locutus est per Prophetas
Et unam sanctam catholicam et apostolicam Ecclesiam
Confiteor unum baptisma in remissionem peccatorum

Christ, the only begotten Son of God. Born of the Father before all ages
God of God,
Light of Light
True God of true God
Begotten, not made, of one substance with the Father; by whom all things were made.
Who for us men and for our salvation came down from heaven.

And he became flesh by the Holy Spirit of the Virgin Mary: and was made man.
He was also crucified for us, suffered under Pontius Pilate, and he was buried.
And on the third day he rose again, according to the Scriptures
He ascended into heaven and sits at the right hand of the Father
He will come again in glory to judge the living and the dead; and of his kingdom there will be no end.
And I believe in the Holy Spirit, the Lord and the Giver of Life
Who proceeds from the Father and the Son
Who together with the Father and the Son is adored and glorified
And who spoke through the Prophets
And one Holy, Catholic and Apostolic Church
I confess one baptism for the forgiveness of sins

Et exspecto resurrectionem mortuorum	And I await the resurrection of the dead
Et vitam venturi saeculi.	And the life of the world to come.
Amen.	Amen.

THE ATHANASIAN SYMBOL

Quicumque vult salus esse, ante omnia opus est ut teneat catholicam fidem:	Whosoever desires to be saved, above all things it is necessary that he hold the Catholic faith,
Quam nisi quisque integram inviolatamque servaverit, absque dubio in aeternum peribit.	Which unless every man keep whole and inviolate, without doubt he will perish forever.
Fides autem catholica haec est: ut unum Deum in Trinitate, et Trinitatem in unitate veneremur.	But the Catholic faith is this: that we worship one God in the Trinity and the Trinity in unity.
Neque confundentes personas, neque substantiam separantes.	Neither confusing the Persons, nor dividing the substance.
Alia est enim persona Patris, alia Filii, alia Spiritus Sancti:	For one is the Person of the Father, another that of the Son, another that of the Holy Ghost.
Sed Patris, et Filii, et Spiritus Sancti una est divinitas, aequalis gloria, coaeterna maiestas.	But there is only one divinity of the Father and of the Son and of the Holy Ghost, an equal glory and coeternal majesty.
Qualis Pater, talis Filius, talis Spiritus Sanctus.	As the Father is, such the Son, and such the Holy Ghost.
Increatus Pater, increatus Filius, increatus Spiritus Sanctus.	Uncreated is the Father, uncreated the Son, and uncreated is the Holy Ghost.
Immensus Pater, immensus Filius, immensus Spiritus Sanctus.	Infinite is the Father, infinite the Son, and infinite the Holy Ghost.
Aeternus Pater, aeternus Filius, aeternus Spiritus Sanctus. Et tamen non tres aeterni, sed unus aeternus.	Eternal is the Father, eternal the Son, and eternal the Holy Ghost. And yet they are not three eternals, but one eternal.

Sicut non tres increati, nec tres immensi, sed unus increatus, et unus immensus.	Just as they are not three uncreated, nor three infinites, but one uncreated and one infinite.
Similiter omnipotens Pater, omnipotens Filius, omnipotens Spiritus Sanctus.	Likewise the Father is almighty, the Son almighty and the Holy Ghost almighty.
Et tamen non tres omnipotentes, sed unus omnipotens.	And yet they are not three almighties, but one almighty.
Ita Deus Pater, Deus Filius, Deus Spiritus Sanctus.	So the Father is God, the Son is God, and the Holy Ghost is God.
Et tamen non tres Dei, sed unus est Deus.	And yet they are not three Gods, but one God.
Ita Dominus Pater, Dominus Filius, Dominus Spiritus Sanctus.	So the Father is Lord, the Son is Lord, and the Holy Ghost is Lord.
Et tamen non tres Domini, sed unus est Dominus.	And yet they are not three Lords, but one Lord.
Quia, sicut singillatim unamquamque personam Deum ac Dominum confiteri christiana veritate compellimur; ita tres Deos aut Dominos dicere catholica religione prohibemur.	For as we are constrained by Catholic truth to confess that each single Person is God and Lord, so are we forbidden by the Catholic religion to say there are three Gods or Lords.
Pater a nullo est factus: nec creatus, nec genitus.	The Father is made by none, neither created nor begotten.
Filius a Patre solo est: non factus, nec creatus, sed genitus.	The Son is of the Father only, not made nor begotten.
Spiritus Sanctus a Patre et Filio: non factus, nec creatus, nec genitus, sed procedens.	The Holy Ghost is from the Father and the Son, not made, nor created, nor begotten but proceeding.
Unus ergo Pater, non tres Patres: unus Filius, non tres Filii: unus Spiritus Sanctus, non tres Spiritus Sancti.	So there is one Father, not three Fathers; one Son, and not three Sons; one Holy Ghost, not three Holy Ghosts.
Et in hac Trinitate nihil prius aut posterius, nihil maius aut minus: sed totae tres personae coaeternae sibi sunt et coaequales.	And in this Trinity there is nothing before or after, nothing greater or less, but all three Persons are coeternal and coequal to each other.

Ita ut per omnia, sicut iam supra dictum est, et unitas in Trinitate, et Trinitas in unitate veneranda sit.	So that in all things, as has been said before, we must worship unity in the Trinity and the Trinity in unity.
Qui vult ergo salvus esse, ita de Trinitate sentiat.	He therefore who desires to be saved, must think thus about the Trinity.
Sed necessarium est ad aeternam salutem, ut Incarnationem quoque Domini nostri Jesu Christi fideliter credat.	But it is necessary for eternal salvation, that he faithfully believe in the Incarnation of our Lord Jesus Christ.
Est ergo fides recta, ut credamus et confiteamur, quia Dominus noster Jesus Christus, Dei Filius, Deus et homo est.	For this is the right faith: that we believe and confess, that our Lord Jesus Christ, the Son of God, is both God and man.
Deus est ex substantia Patris ante saecula genitus: et homo est ex substantia matris in saeculo natus.	He is God of the substance of the Father, begotten before all ages, and He is man of the substance of His mother, born in time.
Perfectus Deus, perfectus homo: ex anima rationali et humana carne subsistens.	Perfect God and perfect man, subsisting with a rational soul and human flesh.
Aequalis Patri secundum divinitatem: minor Patre secundum humanitatem.	Equal to the Father according to His divinity, less than the Father according to His humanity.
Qui, licet Deus sit homo, non duo tamen, sed unus est Christus.	Who, although He is God and man, yet is not two, but one Christ.
Unus autem non conversione divinitatis in carnem, sed assumptione humanitatis in Deum.	One, however, not by any change of divinity into flesh, but by taking up of humanity into God.
Unus omnino, non confusione substantiae, sed unitate personae.	One, indeed, not by a merging of substance, but because of the unity of Person.
Nam sicut anima rationalis et caro unus est homo, ita Deus et homo unus est Christus. Qui passus est pro salute nostra: descendit ad inferos: tertia die resurrexit a mortuis.	For as the rational soul and flesh is one man, so God and man is one Christ. Who suffered for our salvation, descended into hell, on the third day rose from the dead.

Ascendit ad caelos, sedet ad dexteram Dei Patris omnipotentis: inde venturus est judicare vivos et mortuos.	Ascended into heaven, sitteth at the right hand of God the Father almighty, whence He shall come to judge the living and the dead.
Ad cuius adventum omnes homines resurgere habent cum corporibus suis: et reddituri sunt de factis propriis rationem.	At whose coming all men shall rise with their bodies, and give an account of their own works.
Et qui bone egerunt, ibunt in vitam aeternam: qui vero mala, in ignem aeternum.	And those who have done good, shall enter eternal life, while those who did evil, everlasting fire.
Haec est fides catholica, quam nisi quisque fideliter firmiterque crediterit, salvus esse non poterit.	That is the Catholic faith: which unless every man faithfully and firmly believe he cannot be saved.